Washington State Bed & Breakfast Cookbook

Washington State Bed & Breakfast Cookbook

Second Edition

Design: Ole Sykes and Lisa & Marla Bachar
Cover Location: Highland Inn, Friday Harbor, WA
Editing: Melissa Craven, Janis Judd & Nikki Van Thiel

ISBN 1-889593-05-2

Library of Congress Catalog Card Number: 98-065469

Printed in China

3D Press, Inc.
4340 E. Kentucky Ave., Suite 446
Denver, CO 80246
303-300-4484 (phone)
303-300-4494 (fax)
info@3dpress.net (email)

888-456-3607 (order toll-free)
www.3dpress.net

To our husbands,

Rod and Don,

With Love

Acknowledgements

Creating a book is a work involving many people. We owe a great deal of gratitude to the following friends, family members and business colleagues for their support, inspiration, enthusiasm, time and talents:

Melissa Craven, Erin Faino, Janis Judd, Jory Payne, Nikki Van Thiel, our official taste-testers and a special thank you to the owners, innkeepers and chefs of the 72 Washington bed and breakfasts and country inns who generously and enthusiastically shared their favorite recipes and beautiful artwork.

We want to express our love and heartfelt thanks to our parents, Margaret and Harold McCollum and Nan and Lawrence Kaitfors; our husbands, Rod Faino and Don Hazledine; and children, Kyle, Erin, Ryan and daughter-in-law Laura Faino, for their continued interest, ideas, feedback and support.

Table of Contents

Introduction

Many exciting events have occurred since we first published the *Washington State Bed & Breakfast Cookbook* back in 1998. Because of our never-waning fascination with B&Bs, we have continued to visit charming bed and breakfasts and country inns across the country and have tested hundreds of new recipes. The results are two beautiful additions to our cookbook and travel guide series: the *Colorado Bed & Breakfast Cookbook, Second Edition* and the *California Wine Country Bed & Breakfast Cookbook and Travel Guide*.

However, change has also occurred here in Washington. Each year numerous innkeepers retire, yet at the same time, many newcomers to the industry are enthusiastically embracing new careers as professional innkeepers, and sometimes even take on the additional challenge of building their own "dream inn."

We decided the time was right to update and revise our first edition of the *Washington State Bed & Breakfast Cookbook*. We added 12 wonderful new inns and 31 of their tempting recipes, and enhanced the B&B informational categories, which now include handicapped accessibility and willingness to accommodate guests' special dietary needs. Proudly, we present our fifth book, the *Washington State Bed & Breakfast Cookbook, Second Edition*.

We eagerly look forward to starting the next book in our B&B series. Each state provides an exciting new adventure for us, as we discover more B&B treasures and learn about the popular foods of each region. We have come to the conclusion, however, that some things never change. Wherever we go, two things remain constant: Innkeepers are very interesting people, and they delight in serving beautiful and bountiful meals!

We love sharing what we learn. We hope you find this second edition as useful as the first when planning your travels to Washington State's finest B&Bs and in recreating memorable dining moments using this treasure trove of recipes.

Happy Cooking!

Carol Faino & Doreen Hazledine

Breads & Muffins

Breads

&

Muffins

Ravenscroft

Located high on a bluff, the Ravenscroft Inn overlooks Port Townsend Bay, Admiralty Inlet and the Cascade Mountains. Built in 1987 as a replica of a historic Charleston Single House, guests enjoy spacious rooms, private fireplaces and verandas.

The multi-course breakfast, that includes fresh fruit, frappe, homemade muffins, coffeecake and a special entrée, is a gourmet's delight.

INNKEEPERS:	Tim and Gay Stover
ADDRESS:	533 Quincy Street
	Port Townsend, WA 98368
TELEPHONE:	(360) 385-2784; (800) 782-2691
E-MAIL:	info@ravenscroftinn.com
WEBSITE:	www.ravenscroftinn.com
ROOMS:	6 Rooms; 2 Suites; All with private baths
CHILDREN:	Children age 14 and older are welcome
ANIMALS:	Not allowed
HANDICAPPED:	Not handicapped accessible
DIETARY NEEDS:	Will accommodate guests' special dietary needs

Carrot-Zucchini Bread
à la Ravenscroft

Makes 2 Loaves

3	eggs
1¾	cups sugar
1	cup vegetable oil
2	teaspoons vanilla
2⅓	cups flour
2	teaspoons baking soda
¼	teaspoon baking powder
1	teaspoon salt
1	teaspoon cinnamon
1½	cups grated zucchini, drained (squeeze out moisture)
1½	cups grated carrots
1	cup chopped nuts
½	cup raisins, chocolate chips or coconut (optional)

Preheat oven to 350°F. Coat two 9x5-inch loaf pans with nonstick cooking spray. In a large bowl, combine eggs, sugar, oil and vanilla. Sift in flour, baking soda, baking powder, salt and cinnamon; mix well. Stir in zucchini, carrots, nuts and raisins, chocolate chips or coconut, if desired.

Divide batter evenly between the pans. Bake for about 60 minutes, or until a toothpick inserted in center of loaves comes out clean. Cool for about 10 minutes on a wire rack before removing loaves from pans.

Chambered Nautilus

The Chambered Nautilus Bed and Breakfast, named for the beautiful Pacific seashell, was built in 1915 by Herbert and Annie Gowen. Dr. Gowen was among the early faculty at the University of Washington where he founded the department of Oriental Studies.

This elegant Georgian Colonial home is located on a peaceful hill just ten minutes from downtown Seattle and a short walk from the University of Washington campus.

INNKEEPERS:	Joyce Schulte & Steven Poole
ADDRESS:	5005 22nd Avenue NE
	Seattle, WA 98105
TELEPHONE:	(206) 522-2536; (800) 545-8459
E-MAIL:	stay@chamberednautilus.com
WEBSITE:	www.chamberednautilus.com
ROOMS:	10 Rooms; 4 Suites; All with private baths
CHILDREN:	Call ahead
ANIMALS:	Not allowed
HANDICAPPED:	Not handicapped accessible
DIETARY NEEDS:	Will accommodate guests' special dietary needs

Cranberry-Orange Bread

Makes 1 Loaf

"This is a great year-round treat. Buy the cranberries fresh when in season and freeze to use later. Traditionally a holiday item, guests love to be surprised with warm cranberry bread on the breakfast table in the middle of summer." ~ Joyce Schulte, Chambered Nautilus

2	tablespoons butter (or margarine), room temperature
1	egg
1	cup sugar
¾	cup orange juice
¼	teaspoon orange extract
2	cups flour
1	teaspoon baking powder
½	teaspoon baking soda
½	teaspoon salt
2	cups whole fresh cranberries, or frozen, thawed
½	cup chopped walnuts

Preheat oven to 350°F. Grease a 9x5-inch loaf pan. In a large bowl, combine butter, egg and sugar; mix well. Add orange juice and orange extract. Sift in flour, baking powder, baking soda and salt. Stir until just moistened. Fold in cranberries and nuts.

Spoon batter into loaf pan. Bake for approximately 60 minutes, or until a toothpick inserted in center of loaf comes out clean. Cool on wire rack for 10-20 minutes before removing loaf from pan.

Duffy House

Hospitality is an art at the Duffy House Bed and Breakfast Inn. Located near Friday Harbor, it commands a splendid view of Griffin Bay and the snow-capped Olympic Mountains.

This fully-restored, 1920s Tudor-style home exudes warmth and comfort for its guests. A mooring buoy is available off the beach in front of the house.

INNKEEPERS:	Arthur Miller
ADDRESS:	4214 Pear Point Road
	Friday Harbor, WA 98250
TELEPHONE:	(360) 378-5604; (800) 972-2089
E-MAIL:	duffyhouse@rockisland.com
WEBSITE:	www.duffyhouse.com
ROOMS:	5 Rooms; All with private baths
CHILDREN:	Call ahead
ANIMALS:	Not allowed
HANDICAPPED:	Not handicapped accessible
DIETARY NEEDS:	Will accommodate guests' special dietary needs

Prune Bread

Makes 2 Loaves

1	cup pitted prunes
3	eggs
2	cups sugar
1	cup vegetable oil
1	cup buttermilk
2¼	cups flour
1	teaspoon baking soda
1	teaspoon cinnamon
1	teaspoon nutmeg
1	teaspoon allspice
1	cup chopped nuts

Whipped cream, cream cheese or lemon curd (optional)

In a small saucepan, cover the prunes with water. Simmer for about 15 minutes. Drain prunes, then purée in a blender or food processor.

Preheat oven to 350°F. Grease and flour two 9x5-inch loaf pans. In a large bowl, combine eggs, sugar, oil, buttermilk and prune purée. Sift together flour, baking soda, cinnamon, nutmeg and allspice. Toss nuts in the flour/spice mixture to coat nuts. Stir all ingredients together until just moistened. Spoon batter into prepared loaf pans.

Bake for about 60 minutes, or until a toothpick inserted in center of loaves comes out clean. Let cool on a wire rack for 10-20 minutes before removing bread from pans. Let set for awhile, then slice and serve warm. Whipped cream, softened cream cheese or lemon curd are nice accompaniments.

Home by the Sea

Overlooking a wildlife sanctuary, Home by the Sea Bed and Breakfast is located on picturesque Whidbey Island. The Sandpiper Suite offers a private garden entrance, kitchen, dining and living room areas, woodburning stove, outdoor Jacuzzi and a private deck.

Home by the Sea was the first bed and breakfast on Whidbey Island.

INNKEEPERS:	Linda Drew Walsh
ADDRESS:	2388 East Sunlight Beach Road
	Clinton, WA 98236
TELEPHONE:	(360) 321-2964
E-MAIL:	info@homebytheseacottages.com
WEBSITE:	www.homebytheseacottages.com
ROOMS:	1 Suite; 1 Room; Both with private baths
CHILDREN:	Welcome
ANIMALS:	Cats and dogs welcome
HANDICAPPED:	Suite is handicapped accessible
DIETARY NEEDS:	Will accommodate guests' special dietary needs

Jenny's Norwegian Brown Bread

Makes 3 Loaves (or 9 Small Loaves)

"My grandmother Jenny brought this recipe (in her head) from Norway in 1914. When I asked her for the recipe, she said, 'A pan of water, a sifter of flour, etc.' I had to measure out this final recipe. This bread slices nicely for Christmas plates with doilies. Or wrap it in plastic wrap with ribbon and a bow for gift giving. Five generations of our family now bake this bread." ~ Sharon Fritts Drew, Home by the Sea

3½	cups sugar
4	cups water
1	(15-ounce) box raisins
2	cups cold water
¾	cup shortening
2	tablespoons baking soda
1	teaspoon salt
2	teaspoons ground cloves
1	teaspoon cinnamon, or more to taste
7	cups flour
1	cup chopped nuts

Maraschino cherries or candied mixed fruit (optional)

Preheat oven to 375°F. Grease three 9x5-inch loaf pans (or nine 5x3-inch pans). In a very large saucepan or stockpot, mix sugar and the 4 cups of water. Add raisins and bring to a boil. Simmer for about 10 minutes to plump raisins. Remove from heat. Stir in the 2 cups cold water, shortening, baking soda, salt, cloves and cinnamon; mix well. Add flour and mix until all ingredients are thoroughly combined. Add nuts.

Pour batter into prepared loaf pans. (If desired, top with maraschino cherries or candied mixed fruit at Christmas.) Bake regular size (9x5-inch) loaves for approximately 60 minutes (or bake small (5x3-inch) loaves for approximately 25 minutes).

Holly Hedge House

B lending coziness and charm, the Holly Hedge House Bed and Breakfast offers the unassuming elegance of a bygone era. Located less than ten minutes from SeaTac Airport and 15 minutes from the downtown Seattle area, this unique getaway is within walking distance of restaurants, antique shops and outdoor water sports.

Guests enjoy jogging and biking trails along the picturesque Cedar River.

INNKEEPERS:	Lynn & Marian Thrasher
ADDRESS:	908 Grant Avenue South
	Renton, WA 98055
TELEPHONE:	(425) 226-2555; (888) 226-2555
E-MAIL:	holly@hollyhedgehouse.com
WEBSITE:	www.hollyhedgehouse.com
ROOMS:	1 Cottage; Private bath
CHILDREN:	Children age 12 and older are welcome
ANIMALS:	Not allowed; Resident dog
HANDICAPPED:	Not handicapped accessible
DIETARY NEEDS:	Will accommodate guests' special dietary needs

Banana Oatmeal Chocolate Chip Muffins

Makes 12 Muffins

A delicious and creative way to use leftover cooked oatmeal! These muffins are very moist.

½   cup shortening
1   cup sugar
1   egg
1   teaspoon vanilla
2   ripe bananas, mashed
1   cup cooked oatmeal
2   cups flour
1   teaspoon baking soda
½   teaspoon salt
½   cup mini chocolate chips

Preheat oven to 350°F. Grease 12 muffin cups. In a large bowl, cream together shortening, sugar, egg and vanilla. Add mashed bananas and cooked oatmeal. Sift in flour, baking soda and salt. Stir just until dry ingredients are moistened. Stir in chocolate chips.

Spoon batter into prepared muffin cups. Bake for 22-25 minutes, or until done. Cool on a wire rack for 10-15 minutes, then remove muffins from pans. Good served warm or cold.

Quimper Inn

Built by Henry Morgan in 1888 as a simple, two-bedroom home, the Quimper Inn was refurbished in 1904 by Harry and Gertrud Barthrop. Harry and Gertie's Suite, named after the Barthrops, features breathtaking views of the Olympic Mountains, Port Townsend Bay, Admiralty Inlet and Jefferson County's 100-year-old clock tower.

This grand home is located within walking distance of historic Port Townsend.

INNKEEPERS:	Sue & Ron Ramage
ADDRESS:	1306 Franklin Street
	Port Townsend, WA 98368
TELEPHONE:	(360) 385-1060; (800) 557-1060
E-MAIL:	thequimps@olympus.net
WEBSITE:	Not Available
ROOMS:	5 Rooms; 1 Suite; Private and shared baths
CHILDREN:	Children age 12 and older are welcome
ANIMALS:	Not allowed
HANDICAPPED:	Not handicapped accessible
DIETARY NEEDS:	Will accommodate guests' special dietary needs

Banana Blueberry Muffins

Makes 12 Muffins

"I devised this muffin recipe for the growing number of guests who request low-fat foods." ~ Sue Ramage, Quimper Inn. To vary the recipe in the fall, try substituting cranberries for the blueberries and add ½ cup of chopped walnuts.

2	large, ripe bananas, mashed
½	cup non-fat banana yogurt
1	egg, beaten
1½	cups flour
¾	cup sugar
1½	teaspoons baking soda
1	cup blueberries, fresh or frozen (unthawed)

Preheat oven to 350°F. Grease 12 muffin cups. In a large bowl, combine mashed bananas, yogurt and egg; mix completely. Add the flour, sugar and baking soda; stir just until dry ingredients are moistened. Gently fold in blueberries. Spoon batter into prepared muffin cups, about ¾-full. Bake for approximately 30 minutes, or until tops of muffins are golden brown. Cool on a wire rack for 10 minutes before removing muffins from pan.

Carol's Corner

I used fat-free banana cream pie flavored yogurt to test this recipe and the muffins were great! If you are using frozen blueberries, do not let them thaw. If they are icy, quickly rinse them with cold water and pat dry with paper towels (do this just before adding them to the batter – it helps prevent discoloring the batter).

Spring Bay Inn

S pring Bay Inn on Orcas Island is a secluded retreat that rests quietly on its own spectacular water frontage. Over 250 custom windows tempt guests to stay inside to enjoy views of the water and forest.

High ceilings, Rumford fireplaces and walls lined with musical instruments provide a feeling of informal elegance.

INNKEEPERS:	Carl Burger & Sandy Playa
ADDRESS:	464 Spring Bay Trail
	Olga, Orcas Island WA 98279
TELEPHONE:	(360) 376-5531
E-MAIL:	info@springbayinn.com
WEBSITE:	www.springbayinn.com
ROOMS:	5 Rooms; All with private baths
CHILDREN:	Welcome (Must be over age 10 to kayak)
ANIMALS:	Not allowed
HANDICAPPED:	Not handicapped accessible
DIETARY NEEDS:	Will accommodate guests' special dietary needs

Ginger Apple Muffins

Makes 24 Muffins

These are wonderful served warm from the oven.

1	cup milk
⅔	cup butter, melted and cooled
2	eggs, lightly beaten
2	teaspoons vanilla
3½	cups flour
1	cup sugar
1¾	tablespoons baking powder
½	teaspoon salt
½	teaspoon nutmeg
1½	teaspoons ground ginger
2	apples, peeled and diced

Preheat oven to 400°F. Grease muffin cups or use paper liners. In a large bowl, combine milk, melted butter, eggs and vanilla. Combine dry ingredients and mix with apples. Add dry ingredients to wet ingredients and blend together, using as few strokes as possible. Spoon batter into prepared muffin pans, about ⅔-full. Bake for 15-20 minutes.

> *Carol's Corner*
> *Leftover batter can be stored in the refrigerator overnight and baked the next day. Bring batter to room temperature (do not stir) and spoon into muffin cups.*

Caswell's on the Bay

S ituated on three and one-half secluded acres at the edge of Willapa Bay, Caswell's on the Bay Bed and Breakfast Inn offers the ambiance of yesteryear. The five spacious, antique-appointed rooms feature queen-sized beds and private sitting areas.

"Staying here was like checking into heaven." ~ Guest, Caswell's on the Bay

INNKEEPERS:	Bob & Marilyn Caswell
ADDRESS:	25204 Sandridge Road
	Ocean Park, WA 98640
TELEPHONE:	(360) 665-6535; (888) 553-2319
E-MAIL:	bcaswell@willapabay.org
WEBSITE:	www.caswellsinn.com
ROOMS:	5 Rooms; All with private baths
CHILDREN:	Children age 12 and older are welcome
ANIMALS:	Not allowed
HANDICAPPED:	Not handicapped accessible
DIETARY NEEDS:	Will accommodate guests' special dietary needs

Sour Cream Apple-Cranberry Muffins

Makes 18 Muffins

2	cups unbleached, all-purpose flour
¾	cup sugar
1	tablespoon baking powder
¾	teaspoon baking soda
1	teaspoon cinnamon
¼	teaspoon nutmeg
¼	teaspoon allspice
¼	teaspoon ground cloves
¼	teaspoon salt
1	cup dried cranberries
2	eggs, beaten
½	stick (¼ cup) butter, melted
1½	cups low-fat or non-fat sour cream
1	cup peeled and chopped Granny Smith apples

Topping (recipe follows)

Preheat oven to 375°F. Coat muffin pans with nonstick cooking spray. In a large bowl, combine flour, sugar, baking powder, baking soda, cinnamon, nutmeg, allspice, cloves, salt and cranberries; set aside. In a small bowl, combine eggs, melted butter, sour cream and apples. Make a well in dry ingredients. Pour wet ingredients into well; mix just until blended. Fill muffin cups ⅔-full. Sprinkle about 1 teaspoon of topping over each muffin. Bake for 15-20 minutes, or until a toothpick inserted in the center of a muffin comes out clean. Let cool about 5 minutes before removing.

Topping:

¼	cup brown sugar
3	tablespoons flour
2	tablespoons chilled butter

Mix brown sugar and flour. Cut in butter until mixture is crumbly.

Chambered Nautilus

Perched on a peaceful hill in Seattle's University district, the Chambered Nautilus Bed and Breakfast Inn is an elegant 1915 Georgian Colonial home. Located ten minutes from downtown Seattle, this lovely inn offers large guest rooms, attractive gardens and views of the Cascade Mountains.

Amenities include fresh flowers, bottled water, soft robes and a resident teddy bear.

INNKEEPERS:	Joyce Schulte & Steven Poole
ADDRESS:	5005 22nd Avenue NE
	Seattle, WA 98105
TELEPHONE:	(206) 522-2536; (800) 545-8459
E-MAIL:	stay@chamberednautilus.com
WEBSITE:	www.chamberednautilus.com
ROOMS:	10 Rooms; 4 Suites; All with private baths
CHILDREN:	Call ahead
ANIMALS:	Not allowed
HANDICAPPED:	Not handicapped accessible
DIETARY NEEDS:	Will accommodate guests' special dietary needs

Rosemary Buttermilk Muffins

Makes 12 Muffins

These are delicious, savory muffins. For a light texture, gently spoon the dough into the muffin cups and avoid pressing the dough down.

2	cups unbleached, all-purpose flour
2	tablespoons sugar
4	teaspoons baking powder
½	teaspoon baking soda
½	teaspoon salt
½	teaspoon onion powder
1	teaspoon dried rosemary, crushed
½	cup shortening, melted
1	cup buttermilk
2	tablespoons grated Parmesan cheese

Position rack in center of oven. Preheat oven to 400°F. Grease muffin cups. In a large bowl, sift together flour, sugar, baking powder, baking soda, salt and onion powder. Stir in crushed rosemary. Make a well in center of dry ingredients; set aside.

In a medium bowl, whisk melted shortening with buttermilk; beat thoroughly. Pour into well of dry ingredients, stirring only until flour is moistened. Divide batter evenly between muffin cups. Sprinkle Parmesan cheese over the batter in each muffin cup. Bake for 15 minutes, or until golden brown. Cool for 5 minutes in the pan before turning onto wire rack. Serve warm.

❧

Biscuits, Rolls, Coffee Cakes & Scones

❧

Biscuits, Rolls, Coffee Cakes & Scones

White Rose Inn

B uilt in 1922 by Axel G. Hanson, owner of the White River Lumber Company, the White Rose Inn is a 22-room colonial mansion that was constructed with beautiful Honduran mahogany, quarter sawn oak and other elegant accents.

The refined and spacious first floor reception room features a coved ceiling and is perfect for weddings, meetings, banquets and other special functions.

INNKEEPERS:	Eleanor Ludwig
ADDRESS:	1610 Griffin Avenue
	Enumclaw, WA 98022
TELEPHONE:	(360) 825-7194; (800) 404-7194
E-MAIL:	innkeeper@whiteroseinnbb.com
WEBSITE:	www.whiteroseinnbb.com
ROOMS:	4 Rooms; All with private baths
CHILDREN:	Welcome
ANIMALS:	Not allowed
HANDICAPPED:	Not handicapped accessible
DIETARY NEEDS:	Will accommodate guests' special dietary needs

Apricot Pillows

Makes 10 biscuits

These biscuits are good to serve with scrambled eggs and bacon. To save time, prepared fillings such as jam, preserves or apple butter can be substituted for the apricot filling. Use several different flavors of jam to give your guests a choice.

Apricot Filling:
2   cups chopped fresh apricots
⅓   cup sugar
2   tablespoons water

Biscuits:
2   cups flour
¼   cup plus 2 tablespoons sugar
¼   teaspoon cinnamon (may use up to ½ teaspoon)
2   teaspoons baking powder
1   stick (½ cup) butter or margarine, chilled
¼   cup milk
2   eggs, divided

To make apricot filling: In a small saucepan, combine apricots, sugar and water. Simmer over medium heat until thickened, about 15 minutes; set aside.

Preheat oven to 400°F. Line a baking sheet with foil; grease foil. In a large bowl, sift together flour, ¼ cup sugar, cinnamon and baking powder. Using a pastry blender, cut butter into flour mixture until coarse crumbs form. In a small bowl, mix milk and 1 egg. Add to flour mixture and stir until dough forms (if dough is too dry, add a bit more milk).

Divide dough in half. On a lightly floured surface, roll half the dough into a 10x8-inch rectangle. Cut into 5 (2x8-inch) strips. Spread 1 tablespoon apricot filling or jam down center of each strip to within ½ inch of all edges. Fold dough in half to form a "pillow." Pinch edges together (press with fork tines for a decorative edge). Repeat with other half of dough. Beat the other egg and brush pillow tops with it. Sprinkle pillow tops with the 2 tablespoons of sugar. Bake biscuits for 12-15 minutes, until golden. Transfer to wire rack. Serve warm or cold.

Tudor Inn

B uilt in 1910, the Tudor Inn Bed and Breakfast is of English Tudor design. The living room and library invite guests to relax, read or enjoy conversation. Views from the balcony include the Olympic Mountains and the Strait of Juan de Fuca. Breakfast is served in the formal dining room.

Outdoor sports aficionados can enjoy cross-country skiing at nearby Hurricane Ridge.

INNKEEPERS:	Betsy Reed-Schultz
ADDRESS:	1108 South Oak Street
	Port Angeles, WA 98362
TELEPHONE:	(360) 452-3138; (866) 286-2224
E-MAIL:	info@tudorinn.com
WEBSITE:	www.tudorinn.com
ROOMS:	5 Rooms; All with private baths
CHILDREN:	Children age 12 and older are welcome
ANIMALS:	Not allowed
HANDICAPPED:	Not handicapped accessible
DIETARY NEEDS:	Will accommodate guests' special dietary needs

Angel Biscuits

Makes Approximately 24 Biscuits

1	package active dry yeast
2	tablespoons warm water
5	cups flour
1	teaspoon baking soda
1	tablespoon baking powder
1	teaspoon salt
2	tablespoons sugar
2	sticks (1 cup) butter, room temperature plus additional butter (melted) for brushing tops of biscuits before baking
2	cups buttermilk

Preheat oven to 400°F. In a small bowl, dissolve yeast in warm water. Set aside. In a large bowl, sift together flour, baking soda, baking powder, salt and sugar. Cut in the 2 sticks of room temperature butter with pastry blender. Add buttermilk and yeast mixture. Stir until thoroughly moistened. Turn out onto floured board; knead for 1-2 minutes. Roll out to desired thickness and cut into rounds. (If rolled ¾-inch thick and cut with a 2½-inch cutter, yield will be about 24 biscuits.) Brush biscuits with melted butter. Bake on an ungreased cookie sheet for 12-15 minutes.

Blue Heron Inn

S itting at the edge of Silver Lake, the Blue Heron Inn Bed and Breakfast offers a panoramic view of Mount St. Helens and its forested valleys. Located on five acres, this beautiful getaway is perfect for private parties, business meetings and weddings.

Guests relax in the spacious parlor, browse through a fine book selection in the library or lounge on the covered verandah.

INNKEEPERS:	John & Jeanne Robards
ADDRESS:	2846 Spirit Lake Highway
	Castle Rock, WA 98611
TELEPHONE:	(360) 274-9595; (800) 959-4049
E-MAIL:	jeanne@blueheroninn.com
WEBSITE:	www.blueheroninn.com
ROOMS:	7 Rooms; All with private baths
CHILDREN:	Children age 6 and older are welcome
ANIMALS:	Not allowed
HANDICAPPED:	Not handicapped accessible
DIETARY NEEDS:	Will accommodate guests' special dietary needs

Bubble Bread

Makes 8 to 12 Servings

Easy and spectacular – a winner! Note: this bread needs to be assembled a day ahead and rest overnight before baking.

½   cup chopped nuts
24   frozen dough dinner rolls
1   cup brown sugar
1   (3.5-ounce) package butterscotch pudding and pie filling dry mix (do not use instant)
¼   cup sugar
1   teaspoon cinnamon
1½   sticks (¾ cup) butter, melted

Grease and flour (or coat with nonstick cooking spray) a 10-inch Bundt pan. Sprinkle nuts into bottom of pan. Place frozen dinner rolls over nuts; distribute evenly. In a small bowl, mix together brown sugar, pudding mix, sugar and cinnamon; sprinkle over rolls. Pour melted butter over all. Leave pan uncovered on countertop overnight.

Note: You may want to place a cookie sheet under the Bundt pan just in case the rolls spill over a bit during the rising process. This is more likely to happen if your kitchen is very warm.

Next morning: Preheat the oven to 350°F and bake bread for 30 minutes. Cool for 2 minutes. Invert pan onto a rimmed platter, as topping will run.

Rimrock Inn

Named for the rocks that rim the top of Pitcher Canyon, Rimrock Inn Bed and Breakfast is located between Wenatchee and the Mission Ridge ski area.

During one weekend each May, Wenatchee celebrates its heritage in the fruit industry with the Washington State Apple Blossom Festival. Activities include the parades, carnival rides, and art and food in the park.

INNKEEPERS:	Doug & Mary Cook
ADDRESS:	1354 Pitcher Canyon Road
	Wenatchee, WA 98801
TELEPHONE:	(509) 664-5113; (888) 664-5113
E-MAIL:	Not available
WEBSITE:	www.rimrockinn.com
ROOMS:	3 Rooms; All with private baths
CHILDREN:	Children age 10 and older are welcome
ANIMALS:	Not allowed
HANDICAPPED:	Not handicapped accessible
DIETARY NEEDS:	Will accommodate guests' special dietary needs

Sour Cream Orange Rolls

Makes 8 Rolls

1	package active dry yeast
½	cup warm water
1	stick (½ cup) butter, room temperature, divided
2	eggs
½	cup sour cream
3½	cups flour
1	teaspoon salt
2	tablespoons plus ¾ cup sugar
2	tablespoons grated orange zest

Orange icing (recipe follows)

In a large bowl, dissolve yeast in warm water. Add ½ stick butter, eggs, sour cream, flour, salt and the 2 tablespoons of sugar; mix well. Place dough on well-floured board; knead for 5-8 minutes (keep hands and board well floured during the kneading process). Place dough in an oiled bowl; turn dough to coat with oil. Cover with clean towel or plastic wrap; let rise until doubled in size.

In a small bowl, combine the ¾ cup sugar and the orange zest. Set aside. Roll dough into a 10x12-inch rectangle. Spread ½ stick butter over dough. Sprinkle sugar/orange peel mixture over buttered dough. Starting with 12-inch side, roll dough jelly-roll fashion; pinch seam to seal. Cut into 8 rolls (each about 1½ inches thick). Arrange rolls, cut-side down, in a greased 11x7-inch pan. Cover loosely and let rise for 40-45 minutes. Preheat oven to 350°F. Bake rolls for 25 minutes, or until golden. Cool slightly. While rolls are still in pan and warm, glaze with orange icing.

Orange icing:

½	cup sugar
¼	cup sour cream
½	stick (¼ cup) butter
3	tablespoons orange juice

In a medium saucepan over high heat, combine all ingredients. Boil for 3 minutes, stirring occasionally. Cool slightly, then glaze tops of warm rolls.

The Villa

THE VILLA

From its elegant, formal entrance to its beautiful gardens, The Villa Bed and Breakfast captures the charm of an Italian palazzo. With more than 7,000 square feet of space, it possesses a grand elegance.

Every room is full of serendipitous architectural spaces, artfully arranged in cozy nooks and light-filled spaces. A gourmet breakfast of seasonal delights is served each morning.

INNKEEPERS:	Greg & Becky Anglemyer
ADDRESS:	705 North 5th Street
	Tacoma, WA 98403
TELEPHONE:	(253) 572-1157; (888) 572-1157
E-MAIL:	villabb@aol.com
WEBSITE:	www.villabb.com
ROOMS:	6 Rooms; 3 Suites; All with private baths
CHILDREN:	Children age 12 and older are welcome
ANIMALS:	Not allowed
HANDICAPPED:	Is handicapped accessible
DIETARY NEEDS:	Will accommodate guests' special dietary needs

Yogurt Coconut Coffee Cake

Makes 12 Servings

A very moist, flavorful coffee cake. Perfect for your next brunch! This coffee cake can be baked a day in advance. It also freezes well.

1	stick (½ cup) butter, room temperature
½	cup shortening
1	cup sugar
2	eggs
2	cups flour
1	teaspoon baking soda
½	teaspoon salt
1	cup vanilla or plain yogurt
1	teaspoon vanilla

Topping:

⅓	cup sugar
⅓	cup brown sugar
1	teaspoon cinnamon
½	cup coconut

Preheat oven to 350°F. Grease 13x9-inch baking dish. In a large bowl, cream together butter, shortening and sugar. Beat in eggs. In a medium bowl, sift together flour, baking soda and salt. Add to butter mixture. Stir in yogurt and vanilla. Mix well.

In a small bowl, combine topping ingredients; set aside. Drop half of batter by spoonfuls over the bottom of baking dish, then spread evenly on the bottom of the dish. Sprinkle with half of topping. Spoon remaining batter into baking dish and spread carefully. Sprinkle with remaining topping. Bake for 30 minutes, or until a toothpick inserted in center comes out clean (watch carefully so the topping does not burn). Cool on wire rack.

Abendblume Pension

Inspired by the ambiance of fine European country inns, the Abendblume Pension Bed and Breakfast reflects this mood through its carved wood walls, archways, ceilings, deep inset windows and circular stairway.

Guest amenities include Alpine therapeutic massages for two, an outdoor spa, European bedding and luxurious baths with heated tile floors.

INNKEEPERS:	Renee Sexauer
ADDRESS:	12570 Ranger Road
	Leavenworth, WA 98826
TELEPHONE:	(509) 548-4059; (800) 669-7634
EMAIL:	abendblm@rightathome.com
WEBSITE:	www.abendblume.com
ROOMS:	7 Rooms; 4 Suites; All with private baths
CHILDREN:	Not allowed
ANIMALS:	Not allowed
HANDICAPPED:	Not handicapped accessible
DIETARY NEEDS:	Will accommodate guests' special dietary needs

Blueberry Sour Cream Coffee Cake

Makes 12 Servings

2¼ cups flour
2 teaspoons baking powder
½ teaspoon baking soda
½ teaspoon salt
1½ sticks (¾ cup) butter, room temperature
¾ cup sugar
1 teaspoon vanilla
2 eggs
1 cup sour cream
1 cup fresh or frozen blueberries (more or less)
Streusel mixture (recipe follows)

Preheat oven to 350°F. Grease and flour 13x9-inch glass baking dish. In a medium bowl, sift together flour, baking powder, baking soda and salt. Set aside. In a large bowl, cream together butter, sugar and vanilla. Beat in eggs one at a time until fluffy. Add flour mixture to creamed butter/egg mixture alternately with sour cream.

Spread half the batter in the baking dish. Sprinkle with blueberries and half of the streusel mixture. Carefully spoon on remaining batter. Sprinkle with remaining streusel mixture. Bake for approximately 40 minutes, or until a toothpick inserted in center of the cake comes out clean.

Streusel mixture:
⅓ cup flour
1 teaspoon cinnamon
⅔ cup light brown sugar
½ stick (¼ cup) chilled butter
⅔ cup chopped walnuts (may use up to 1 cup)

In a small bowl, combine flour, cinnamon and brown sugar. Using a pastry blender, cut in butter until mixture is crumbly. Stir in walnuts.

Lietz's

Lietz's Bed and Breakfast is a cozy country inn located four and one-half miles east of Leavenworth on the Wenatchee River. Guests savor the delicious, family-style breakfast that is served each morning from seven to ten o'clock.

With the close proximity of the Wenatchee River, guests can experience adventuresome innertube float trips, with innertubes provided by the inn.

INNKEEPERS:	Verne & Helen Lietz
ADDRESS:	8305 Lynn Street
	Peshastin, WA 98847
TELEPHONE:	(509) 548-7504
E-MAIL:	lietzaire@linear.com
WEBSITE:	Not available
ROOMS:	3 Rooms; Shared baths
CHILDREN:	Welcome
ANIMALS:	Not allowed
HANDICAPPED:	Is handicapped accessible
DIETARY NEEDS:	Will accommodate guests' special dietary needs

Rhubarb Coffee Cake

Makes 8 to 12 Servings

This coffee cake also makes a great dessert. Try serving it warm with a big scoop of vanilla ice cream.

1	stick (½ cup) margarine, room temperature
1½	cups brown sugar
1	egg
1	cup sour cream
1	teaspoon baking soda
2	cups flour
½	teaspoon salt
2	cups (½-inch) cubed rhubarb (about ¾ pound)
1	teaspoon vanilla

Topping (recipe follows)

Preheat oven to 350°F. Grease and flour 13x9-inch glass baking dish. In a large bowl, cream together margarine and brown sugar. Add egg and blend well; set aside.

In a medium bowl, combine sour cream and baking soda. Sift flour and salt into margarine/egg mixture alternately with sour cream/baking soda mixture. Add rhubarb and vanilla. Mix well. Spoon batter into baking dish. Sprinkle topping over batter. Bake for approximately 35-40 minutes. Cool on wire rack.

Topping:

½	cup sugar
1	teaspoon cinnamon
1	tablespoon butter
½	cup chopped nuts (optional)

Combine sugar and cinnamon in a small bowl. Cut in butter until a crumbly texture is achieved. Add nuts, if desired.

Camano Island Inn

Camano Island Inn

The Camano Island Inn Bed and Breakfast boasts six deluxe waterfront guestrooms. Amenities include private baths and patios, Jacuzzi tubs and fireplaces. Each room has an unobstructed view of the boat traffic on Saratoga Passage, the Olympic Mountains and fabulous sunsets.

The inn's own apple, pear and prune orchards provide a bounty of fresh fruit used in the breakfasts.

INNKEEPERS:	Jon & Kari Soth
ADDRESS:	1054 South West Camano Drive
	Camano Island, WA 98292
TELEPHONE:	(360) 387-0783; (888) 718-0783
E-MAIL:	reservations@camanoislandinn.com
WEBSITE:	www.camanoislandinn.com
ROOMS:	6 Suites; All with private baths
CHILDREN:	Children age 10 and older are welcome; Call ahead
ANIMALS:	Not allowed
HANDICAPPED:	Is handicapped accessible
DIETARY NEEDS:	Will accommodate guests' special dietary needs

Cranberry-Apple Braid

Makes 8 to 10 Servings

1   (3-ounce) package cream cheese, chilled and cut into pieces
½   stick (¼ cup) butter, chilled and cut into pieces
2   cups baking mix (such as Bisquick)
⅓   cup milk
¾   cup whole berry cranberry sauce
1   large apple, peeled and chopped
1   teaspoon sugar
½   teaspoon cinnamon
Glaze (recipe follows)

Preheat oven to 425°F. Put cream cheese, butter and baking mix into a large bowl. Using a pastry blender, cut until mixture is crumbly. Mix in milk. On a floured piece of waxed paper, knead dough for 1 minute. Roll into a 14x10-inch rectangle. Remove waxed paper and place dough on a greased cookie sheet. Set aside.

In a small bowl, mix cranberry sauce, apple, sugar and cinnamon. Place cranberry mixture in a 3-inch-wide strip, lengthwise, down center of dough. Cut dough on both sides of filling into 1-inch-wide strips, almost to the filling. Alternating from side to side, fold strips over filling at an angle. The end of each strip should be covered by next strip. Pinch dough at both ends to seal. Bake for 15 minutes, or until braid is golden brown. Remove to wire rack. Drizzle glaze over warm braid (place a piece of waxed paper underneath rack to catch drips from the glaze).

Glaze:
1   teaspoon butter, melted
1   tablespoon milk
1   tablespoon cranberry juice
1   cup powdered sugar

In a small bowl, combine melted butter, milk and cranberry juice. Gradually beat in powdered sugar to reach glaze consistency.

Palisades at Dash Point

The Palisades Bed and Breakfast at Dash Point offers a luxurious European-style getaway. Guests enjoy a breathtaking view of Puget Sound and the Olympic Mountain Range from their three-room suite.

Conveniently located between Seattle and Tacoma, this secluded hideaway pampers guests with thick terry robes, a sumptuous breakfast and a licensed "on-call" masseuse.

INNKEEPERS:	Dennis & Peggy LaPorte
ADDRESS:	5162 SW 311th Place
	Federal Way, WA 98023
TELEPHONE:	(253) 838-4376; (888) 838-4376
E-MAIL:	laporte2@ix.netcom.com
WEBSITE:	www.palisadesbb.com
ROOMS:	1 Suite; Private bath
CHILDREN:	Not allowed
ANIMALS:	Not allowed
HANDICAPPED:	Not handicapped accessible
DIETARY NEEDS:	Will accommodate guests' special dietary needs

Blueberry Scones with Vanilla Crème Filling

Makes 8 Scones

2¼   cups flour
1   tablespoon baking powder
½   teaspoon salt
1   stick (½ cup) butter or margarine, chilled
½   cup blueberries
1   egg
¾   cup buttermilk
Sugar, to sprinkle on tops of scones
Vanilla Crème Filling (recipe follows)

Preheat oven to 350°F. In food processor, blend flour, baking powder and salt. Cut in butter or margarine; pulse several times until mixture is crumbly. Transfer to a medium bowl. Add blueberries; toss to coat. Set aside.

In a small bowl, combine egg and buttermilk. Add to flour/blueberry mixture. Stir gently, just until blended. Turn dough onto lightly floured surface and knead lightly a few times. Pat dough into a 6- to 7-inch round. Cut dough into 8 wedges. Transfer to ungreased baking sheet and sprinkle tops of scones with sugar. Bake for 20-25 minutes, or until puffed and golden. Cool on wire rack. Cut each scone in half horizontally and spread Vanilla Crème Filling between top and bottom halves; serve.

Vanilla Crème Filling:
1¼   cups powdered sugar
2   tablespoons butter, room temperature
½   teaspoon vanilla
1   tablespoon milk or half & half

In a small bowl, beat together all ingredients with an electric mixer until smooth. A few more drops of milk may be added if a thinner spreading consistency is desired.

Highland Cottage

Built in 1901, the Highland Cottage Bed and Breakfast was originally the elegant private residence of the distinguished George F. Ward family. The refurbished, eclectic decor features a large and brilliantly colored stained glass window, decorative inlays and antique furnishings.

This traditional Victorian has two spacious upstairs rooms and a self-contained cottage.

INNKEEPERS:	Lon & Ellie Overson
ADDRESS:	622 Highland Avenue
	Bremerton, WA 98337
TELEPHONE:	(360) 373-2235
E-MAIL:	overson@msn.com
WEBSITE:	www.maxrules.com/hild.html
ROOMS:	2 Rooms; 1 Cottage; Private and shared baths
CHILDREN:	Welcome
ANIMALS:	Not allowed
HANDICAPPED:	Call ahead
DIETARY NEEDS:	Will accommodate guests' special dietary needs

Country Scones with Devonshire Cream

Makes 10 Scones

1   egg
Buttermilk (enough to make 1 cup of liquid when combined with egg)
2   cups unbleached, all-purpose flour
¼   cup sugar
2½   teaspoons baking powder
½   teaspoon salt
6   tablespoons (¾ stick) butter, chilled
½   cup raisins or dried cranberries
½   cup white chocolate chips
Devonshire cream (recipe follows)

Preheat oven to 400°F. In a 1-cup measure, slightly beat egg. Add enough buttermilk to make 1 cup of liquid. Set aside.

In a large bowl, sift together flour, sugar, baking powder and salt. Using a pastry blender, cut in butter until mixture is crumbly. Add raisins (or cranberries) and white chocolate chips. Add buttermilk mixture and stir just until dough clings together (do not overmix).

On ungreased baking sheet, drop dough by ¼-cupfuls. Bake for 12-15 minutes, or until lightly browned. Serve with Devonshire cream. Delicious!

Devonshire cream:
1   (3-ounce) package cream cheese, room temperature
1   tablespoon powdered sugar, sifted
½   teaspoon vanilla (or favorite flavoring)
⅓   cup whipping cream (may use up to ½ cup)

In a small bowl, beat together cream cheese, powdered sugar and vanilla until fluffy. Add whipping cream and beat just until spreading consistency (do not overbeat).

Autumn Pond

Surrounded by panoramic views of the majestic Cascades, the Autumn Pond Bed and Breakfast is the perfect getaway for family reunions or small business gatherings. The stunning great room features exposed cedar beams, rough cut cedar paneling and bay windows.

Local activities include golf, horse rides, hayrides, fishing, swimming, mountain biking, white water rafting, hiking and rock climbing.

INNKEEPERS:	John & Jennifer Lorenz
ADDRESS:	10388 Titus Road
	Leavenworth, WA 98826
TELEPHONE:	(509) 548-4482; (800) 222-9661
E-MAIL:	info@autumnpond.com
WEBSITE:	www.autumnpond.com
ROOMS:	5 Rooms; All with private baths
CHILDREN:	Children age 10 and older are welcome
ANIMALS:	Not allowed; Resident dogs
HANDICAPPED:	Not handicapped accessible
DIETARY NEEDS:	Will accommodate guests' special dietary needs

Cranberry Orange Buttermilk Scones

Makes 16 Scones

3	cups unbleached flour
⅓	cup sugar
2½	teaspoons baking powder
½	teaspoon baking soda
¾	teaspoon salt
2	sticks (1 cup) butter, chilled and cut in pieces
1	egg
1	cup buttermilk
¾	cup dried cranberries

Grated zest of 1 large orange
1   teaspoon vanilla
Turbinado or raw sugar for topping

Preheat oven to 400°F. In a large bowl, mix flour, sugar, baking powder, baking soda and salt. With pastry blender or food processor, cut in butter until it has the consistency of coarse crumbs.

In a separate bowl, mix egg, buttermilk, cranberries, orange zest and vanilla. Mix egg mixture into flour mixture until it can be gathered into a ball. Divide ball in half and pat out each half on a floured board until ¾-inch thick. Cut each circle into 8 wedges, then sprinkle tops with raw sugar. Transfer to parchment covered baking sheet. Bake for 15-20 minutes.

Stratford Manor

Situated on 30 acres, the Stratford Manor Bed and Breakfast is a stately, Tudor-style country home. Guests enjoy the solarium, cozy library, enchanting gardens, plush bath robes, soft towels and relaxing massages.

"A wonderful night. Far exceeded our expectations." ~ Guest, Stratford Manor

INNKEEPERS:	Leslie & Jim Lohse
ADDRESS:	4566 Anderson Way
	Bellingham, WA 98226
TELEPHONE:	(360) 715-8441; (800) 240-6779
E-MAIL:	llohse@aol.com
WEBSITE:	www.stratfordmanor.com
ROOMS:	3 Rooms; All with private baths
CHILDREN:	Not allowed
ANIMALS:	Not allowed
HANDICAPPED:	Not handicapped accessible
DIETARY NEEDS:	Will accommodate guests' special dietary needs

Blueberry Scones

Makes 8 Scones

"These are also very tasty with just the orange zest or with fresh cranberries instead of blueberries." ~ Leslie Lohse, Stratford Manor

2	cups flour
¼	cup sugar
1	tablespoon baking powder
¼	teaspoon baking soda
¼	teaspoon salt
1	tablespoon finely grated orange zest (1-2 oranges)
½	stick (¼ cup) butter, chilled
1	cup fresh or frozen blueberries
1	egg
½	cup buttermilk
1	teaspoon vanilla

Preheat oven to 400°F. In a large bowl, sift together flour, sugar, baking powder, baking soda and salt. Add orange zest. Using a pastry blender, cut in butter until mixture resembles coarse crumbs. Add blueberries, tossing to coat. Make a well in center of ingredients; set aside.

In a small bowl, combine egg, buttermilk and vanilla. Pour wet ingredients into the well in dry ingredients, stirring with a fork until just moistened. Turn dough onto lightly floured board and knead lightly into a ball shape. Pat dough into a 7-inch circle and cut into 8 wedges. Transfer to an ungreased baking sheet, leaving 1-2 inches between wedges. Bake for 15-20 minutes, until lightly browned. Serve warm.

Pancakes, Waffles, Crêpes & Blintzes

Pancakes,
Waffles, Crêpes
& Blintzes

A Quail's Roost Inn

Built in 1902, A Quail's Roost Inn Bed and Breakfast has been tastefully restored to capture its turn-of-the-century ambiance and is in the process of being placed on the National Register of Historic Places.

"Best B&B ever! We love it here! The owner is the greatest!" ~ Guest, A Quail's Roost Inn

INNKEEPERS:	Brad Stolzenburg
ADDRESS:	121 East Highland Avenue
	Chelan, WA 98816
TELEPHONE:	(509) 682-2892; (800) 681-2892
E-MAIL:	Not available
WEBSITE:	www.aquailsroostinn.com
ROOMS:	2 Rooms; 1 Suite; All with private baths
CHILDREN:	Children age 10 and older are welcome
ANIMALS:	Not allowed
HANDICAPPED:	Not handicapped accessible
DIETARY NEEDS:	Will accommodate guests' special dietary needs

French Banana Pancakes

1   cup flour
¼   cup powdered sugar
¼   teaspoon salt
1   cup milk
2   eggs
¼   teaspoon vanilla
3   tablespoons butter, melted

Filling:
½   stick (¼ cup) butter
¼   cup brown sugar
¼   teaspoon cinnamon
¼   teaspoon nutmeg
¼   cup light cream
5   firm bananas, halved lengthwise
Whipped cream and additional cinnamon (optional)

In a medium bowl, sift together flour, powdered sugar and salt. Add milk, eggs, vanilla and melted butter. Beat until smooth. Heat a lightly greased 6-inch skillet. Add 3 tablespoons batter to cover bottom of skillet. Cook until lightly browned; turn and brown other side. Remove to a wire rack. Repeat with remaining batter.

To make filling: Melt butter in large skillet. Stir in brown sugar, cinnamon and nutmeg. Add cream and cook until slightly thickened. Add bananas and heat for 2-3 minutes, spooning sauce over them. Remove from heat.

To serve: Roll a pancake around each banana half and place on serving plates. Spoon sauce over pancakes. Top with whipped cream and a dash of cinnamon.

The Victorian

Located in Coupeville on beautiful Whidbey Island, The Victorian Bed and Breakfast is a Registered National Historical Landmark. Guests of this Italianate Victorian home enjoy the charming upstairs bedrooms or the guest cottage.

Called the City of Sea Captains, Coupeville blends its early Indian lore with a unique maritime history and a vigorous pioneer spirit.

INNKEEPERS:	Heide Hennessey & Simon Bargh
ADDRESS:	602 North Main Street
	Coupeville, WA 98239
TELEPHONE:	(360) 678-5305
E-MAIL:	Not available
WEBSITE:	www.whidbeyvictorianbandb.com
ROOMS:	2 Rooms; 1 Cottage; All with private baths
CHILDREN:	Welcome in cottage
ANIMALS:	Allowed in cottage
HANDICAPPED:	Not handicapped accessible
DIETARY NEEDS:	Will accommodate guests' special dietary needs

Apple Pancake

Makes 6 to 8 Servings

8	eggs
1½	cups milk
3	tablespoons sugar
1	teaspoon vanilla
½	teaspoon salt
½	teaspoon cinnamon
2	large Granny Smith apples
1	stick (½ cup) margarine, cut into pieces
1	cup flour
4	tablespoons brown sugar

Preheat oven to 425°F. In a large bowl, mix together eggs, milk, sugar, vanilla, salt and cinnamon. Set aside.

Peel apples and cut into ¼-inch slices. In the oven, melt margarine in a 13x9-inch baking dish (watch carefully so it doesn't burn), then remove from oven. Arrange apple slices in baking dish.

Stir flour into egg/milk mixture to make batter (it will be lumpy). Put dish with margarine and apples into oven until margarine sizzles. Remove dish from oven and pour batter over apples. Sprinkle with brown sugar and return to oven (use pot holders – the baking dish will still be hot). Bake for 25 minutes. Serve immediately.

Otters Pond

Situated on six and one-half acres on breathtaking Orcas Island, the Otters Pond Bed and Breakfast overlooks a 20-acre pond. The pond attracts a multitude of wildlife, including otters, ducks, geese, blue heron, kingfishers, bald eagles and trumpeter swans. Sports enthusiasts enjoy biking, hiking, kayaking, fishing or searching for Orca whales.

Each guest room features original artwork from local artists.

INNKEEPERS:	Carl & Susan Silvernail
ADDRESS:	100 Tomihi Drive; PO Box 1540
	Eastsound, WA 98245
TELEPHONE:	(360) 376-8844; (888) 893-9680
E-MAIL:	host@otterspond.com
WEBSITE:	www.otterspond.com
ROOMS:	5 Rooms; All with private baths
CHILDREN:	Not allowed
ANIMALS:	Not allowed
HANDICAPPED:	Not handicapped accessible
DIETARY NEEDS:	Will accommodate guests' special dietary needs

Great Northwest Apple Pancakes

Makes 10 Pancakes

5	tablespoons butter, melted
1	cup milk
2	eggs
1¼	cups flour
½	teaspoon salt
4	teaspoons baking powder
2	tablespoons sugar
1	teaspoon cinnamon
3-4	Granny Smith Apples, sliced
1	cup coarsely chopped toasted walnuts

Maple syrup
Otters Pond Apple Butter (recipe follows)

In a medium bowl, mix melted butter, milk and eggs. Set aside. In a large bowl, mix flour, salt, baking powder, sugar and cinnamon. Gently add milk/egg mixture to flour mixture; stir only until dry ingredients are moistened. Cook on an oiled, hot griddle or skillet, using ¼ cup batter for each pancake. While cooking, quickly place 3 apple slices on top of each pancake before flipping. When pancake is bubbly, flip over and cook apple side until pancake is cooked. Serve apple-side-up with toasted walnuts, maple syrup and Otters Pond Apple Butter.

Otters Pond Apple Butter:

1¾	cups sugar
4	teaspoons cinnamon
¼	teaspoon ground cloves
¼	teaspoon salt
7	apples (enough to fill a 1½ quart crock pot) peeled and sliced

Combine sugar, cinnamon, cloves and salt. Add apple slices and toss to coat. Put apples in a crock pot and cook on high for 2 hours. Turn to low and cook all day, or until thick and dark in color. Pour apples into sterilized jars and seal or freeze in plastic containers (consult your county extension office for information on canning safety). Makes six 8-ounce jars.

Salisbury House

Salisbury House Bed and Breakfast Inn offers gracious accommodations for the discerning traveler. Situated on a tree-lined residential street, this urban bed and breakfast is only minutes from downtown Seattle, the University of Washington and Seattle University.

The public rooms are large and bright. A well-stocked library has a game table for an evening of chess or a morning of writing postcards by the fire.

INNKEEPERS:	Cathryn & Mary Wiese
ADDRESS:	750 16th Avenue East
	Seattle, WA 98112
TELEPHONE:	(206) 328-8682
E-MAIL:	sleep@salisburyhouse.com
WEBSITE:	www.salisburyhouse.com
ROOMS:	5 Rooms; All with private baths
CHILDREN:	Children age 12 and older are welcome
ANIMALS:	Not allowed
HANDICAPPED:	Not handicapped accessible
DIETARY NEEDS:	Will accommodate guests' special dietary needs

Mary's Oatmeal Pancakes

Makes About 20 (4-inch) Pancakes

For these surprisingly light and fluffy pancakes, the oats soak in buttermilk overnight so they offer body, texture and richness to the batter, without weighing it down. They are delicious served with a side of chunky applesauce.

2	cups rolled oats
3	cups buttermilk
½	cup flour
1	teaspoon baking soda
1	teaspoon baking powder
¼	teaspoon salt
2	eggs, lightly beaten
¼	cup vegetable oil

Maple syrup (topping)
Low-fat sour cream (topping)
Yogurt (topping)
Chunky applesauce

Night before making pancakes: In a large bowl, stir together oats and buttermilk. Cover and refrigerate overnight.

To make pancakes: In a large bowl, combine flour, baking soda, baking powder and salt. Set aside. In a small bowl, stir together eggs and oil. Add egg mixture to flour mixture, followed by oatmeal mixture. Stir gently until thoroughly combined.

Cook pancakes on lightly oiled, hot griddle or skillet until golden brown, about 2 minutes per side. Serve hot, topped with maple syrup, low-fat sour cream and yogurt, and with chunky applesauce on the side.

Blue Heron Inn

Located opposite the Mount St. Helens National Monument, the Blue Heron Inn features seven beautiful rooms with private bathrooms and balconies. Guests relax in the spacious parlor with its breathtaking views of Silver Lake and Mount St. Helens or browse through the library with its fine selection of books and other reading material.

A savory country breakfast and full-course dinner is provided for all guests.

INNKEEPERS:	John & Jeanne Robards
ADDRESS:	2846 Spirit Lake Highway
	Castle Rock, WA 98611
TELEPHONE:	(360) 274-9595; (800) 959-4049
E-MAIL:	jeanne@blueheroninn.com
WEBSITE:	www.blueheroninn.com
ROOMS:	7 Rooms; All with private baths
CHILDREN:	Children age 6 and older are welcome
ANIMALS:	Not allowed; Resident dog
HANDICAPPED:	Is handicapped accessible
DIETARY NEEDS:	Will accommodate guests' special dietary needs

Sourdough Pancakes

Makes 20 (5-inch) Pancakes

This pancake batter needs to be made the night before. No mess and no fuss in the morning. The batter will keep for days.

1	package active dry yeast
¼	cup warm water
1	quart buttermilk
½	cup vegetable oil
1	teaspoon salt
4	tablespoons sugar
1	tablespoon baking soda
4	cups flour
2	tablespoons baking powder
4	eggs, well beaten

In a very large bowl, dissolve yeast in warm water. Stir in buttermilk, oil, salt, sugar and baking soda. Add flour and baking powder; mix well. Fold in eggs. Store in refrigerator overnight in container at least 2 times bigger than amount of mixture. (Don't worry about a dark film that will grow on top of the batter; just be sure to stir it in before using.) The batter will keep in the refrigerator for up to 2 weeks.

To make pancakes: Drop batter by ⅓-cupfuls onto a hot, oiled griddle or skillet. Cook until golden brown on each side.

Inn at Penn Cove

The Inn at Penn Cove Bed and Breakfast consists of two of Coupeville's finest historic homes: the 1887 Kineth House and the 1891 Coupe-Gillespie House. The Italianate Kineth House, listed on the National Historic Registry, has an air of quiet luxury. The Coupe-Gillespie combines a fresh country feel with touches of Oriental beauty.

The inn is located on Whidbey Island, the longest island on the Pacific Coast.

INNKEEPERS:	Mitchell & Gladys Howard
ADDRESS:	702 North Main Street
	Coupeville, WA 98239
TELEPHONE:	(360) 678-8000; (800) 688-2683
E-MAIL:	penncove@whidbey.net
WEBSITE:	www.whidbey.com/penncove
ROOMS:	6 Rooms; Private and shared baths
CHILDREN:	Welcome; Call ahead for guidelines
ANIMALS:	Not allowed
HANDICAPPED:	Not handicapped accessible
DIETARY NEEDS:	Will accommodate guests' special dietary needs

Rice Pancakes

Makes 8 Pancakes

This recipe is simple and can also be modified to meet several unusual diets. It is low in fat and sodium, and the flour can be replaced by rice flour or any gluten-free flour for those who are gluten intolerant.

2	tablespoons flour
1	teaspoon baking powder
2	eggs (if egg-replacers are used, pancakes may not hold together very well)
2	tablespoons skim milk
2	tablespoons canola oil
1½	cups cooked brown rice

In a medium bowl, mix together flour and baking powder. Set aside. In another medium bowl, beat together eggs, milk and oil. Stir in rice. Add wet ingredients to dry ingredients. Mix until combined. Drop batter by ¼-cupfuls onto a hot, oiled griddle or nonstick skillet. Cook until golden brown on each side.

> *Carol's Corner*
> *I tested this recipe using a nonstick skillet. The pancakes browned nicely using no additional oil.*

MacKaye Harbor Inn

The MacKaye Harbor Inn was built in 1904 by the Tralness family. In 1927, while Mr. and Mrs. Tralness visited family in Norway, their teenage children rebuilt the old farmhouse. It became the first home on Lopez Island to have electricity.

Hospitality pervades this island getaway. Mrs. Tralness kept Norwegian cookies in the entry for passersby, and its sandy beach was the site of many island picnics.

INNKEEPERS:	Robin & Mike Bergstrom
ADDRESS:	949 MacKaye, PO Box 1940
	Lopez Island, WA 98261
TELEPHONE:	(360) 468-2253; (888) 314-6140
E-MAIL:	innkeeper@mackayeharborinn.com
WEBSITE:	www.mackayeharborinn.com
ROOMS:	4 Rooms; 1 Suite; 2 Cottages; Private and shared baths
CHILDREN:	Children age 9 and older are welcome
ANIMALS:	Not allowed
HANDICAPPED:	Not handicapped accessible
DIETARY NEEDS:	Will accommodate guests' special dietary needs

Finnish Pancake

Makes 6 to 8 Servings

"This is the recipe that gets the best reviews and, therefore, has become a tradition at the inn. It's almost like having custard for breakfast, something gentle for the awakening tummy and tongue." ~ Robin Bergstrom, MacKaye Harbor Inn

8   eggs
½   teaspoon salt
¼   cup honey
⅔   cup flour
2½   cups milk
½   stick (¼ cup) butter
Suggested toppings: jam, powdered sugar or nutmeg

Preheat oven to 425°F. In a blender, combine eggs, salt and honey. Alternately, add flour and milk, blending after each addition. In the oven, melt the butter in a 13x9-inch baking dish (check butter frequently so it doesn't burn). Pour batter over melted butter in heated baking dish. Return baking dish to oven (the dish will still be hot – be sure to use potholders) and bake for 20-25 minutes, or until puffed and golden. Drizzle with hot, melted jam or sprinkle with powdered sugar or nutmeg.

Marianna Stoltz House

Surrounded by century-old trees, the Marianna Stoltz House Bed and Breakfast was built in 1908. This stately residence displays the best craftsmanship of that era and boasts high ceilings, oriental rugs, fir woodwork, leaded glass and maple floors.

A generous and sumptuous breakfast includes such specialties as Stoltz House strata, puffy Dutch pancakes with homemade apple syrup and peach Melba parfait.

INNKEEPERS:	Phyllis Maguire
ADDRESS:	427 East Indiana
	Spokane, WA 99207
TELEPHONE:	(509) 483-4316; (800) 978-6587
E-MAIL:	info@mariannastoltzhouse.com
WEBSITE:	www.mariannastoltzhouse.com
ROOMS:	4 Rooms; 1 Suite; Private and shared baths
CHILDREN:	Children are welcome
ANIMALS:	Not allowed
HANDICAPPED:	Not handicapped accessible
DIETARY NEEDS:	Will accommodate guests' special dietary needs

Stoltz House Secret Pancakes

Makes 15 to 18 Pancakes

Absolutely delicious! This batter needs to be made the night before. It will keep for a week in the refrigerator. The batter may darken, but this is from the yeast — just stir lightly before cooking. If you cannot find huckleberries for the sauce, you can use blueberries instead.

1	pint low-fat buttermilk
1	tablespoon sugar
½	package active dry yeast
½	teaspoon salt
2	cups flour
1	tablespoon baking soda
1	tablespoon baking powder
2	tablespoons canola oil
5	eggs
½	cup heavy cream

Stoltz House Huckleberry Sauce (recipe follows)
Whipping cream whipped with almond extract

Combine buttermilk, sugar and yeast. Combine salt, flour, baking soda and baking powder. Add to buttermilk mixture; mix well. Stir in oil. Beat eggs with an electric mixer for about 5 minutes, or until light yellow and thickened; carefully fold into buttermilk/flour mixture. Cover and refrigerate overnight.

Next morning, stir in heavy cream. Cook on hot griddle. Top with warm huckleberry sauce and whipped cream flavored with almond extract.

Stoltz House Huckleberry Sauce:

2	cups huckleberries (use blueberries if huckleberries are unavailable)
¾	cup sugar
1	tablespoon lemon juice
2	tablespoons cornstarch
1	cup water (use less if berries are frozen)

Combine huckleberries, sugar and lemon juice in saucepan. Stir over medium-high heat until berries are soft. Mix cornstarch and water; stir into fruit. Cook, stirring occasionally, until slightly thickened. Serve hot.

Trumpeter Inn

The Trumpeter Inn Bed and Breakfast is just one mile from the town of Friday Harbor situated among the rolling hills of the San Juan Valley. This bed and breakfast is a pastoral estate surrounded by ponds and meadows.

Named for the Trumpeter swans that grace the nearby marshlands in winter, the Inn is a perfect retreat for those wishing to enjoy the beauty and peace of the San Juans.

INNKEEPERS:	Mark Zipkin & Aylene Geringer
ADDRESS:	318 Trumpeter Way
	Friday Harbor, WA 98250
TELEPHONE:	(800) 826-7926
E-MAIL:	swan@rockisland.com
WEBSITE:	www.trumpeterinn.com
ROOMS:	6 Rooms; All with private baths
CHILDREN:	Children age 12 and older are welcome
ANIMALS:	Not allowed
HANDICAPPED:	Is handicapped accessible
DIETARY NEEDS:	Will accommodate guests' special dietary needs

Magic Strawberry Pancake Basket

Makes 4 to 6 Servings

You need to start this recipe 1 to 2 hours before serving.

Strawberry sour cream filling:

3   pints strawberries, stems removed and halved
½   cup powdered sugar
2   cups sour cream
¼   cup brown sugar

Stir together strawberries and powdered sugar; set aside. Mix sour cream and brown sugar. Refrigerate for 1-2 hours, until ready to use.

Pancake basket:

2   eggs
½   cup milk
¼   teaspoon salt, or to taste
½   cup flour
1   tablespoon butter or margarine

Place oven rack in center of oven and preheat oven to 450°F. In a small bowl, mix eggs, milk, salt and flour. Put butter in pie or quiche dish (I like to use individual ramekins). Place in oven for 2 minutes, or until butter is melted. Swirl to coat bottom and immediately pour in egg batter. Bake for 15 minutes. Lower oven temperature to 350°F and bake for 8-10 minutes more, or until puffed and golden brown.

Remove dishes from oven. Lift out pancake baskets and place on serving plates. Spoon strawberries in the center and top with chilled sour cream. If made in a pie dish, cut into wedges to serve.

Kangaroo House

B uilt in 1907, the Kangaroo House has operated as a bed and breakfast
since 1981. Guests find a restful haven of lovely gardens, delicious
breakfasts and delightfully decorated and comfortable rooms.

Breakfast ingredients include local specialties and the freshest seasonal
fruits, vegetables and garden herbs. All breads, pastries and muffins are
baked in the Kangaroo House kitchen.

INNKEEPERS:	Peter & Helen Allen
ADDRESS:	1459 North Beach Road, PO Box 334
	Eastsound, WA 98245
TELEPHONE:	(360) 376-2175; (888) 371-2175
E-MAIL:	innkeeper@kangaroohouse.com
WEBSITE:	www.kangaroohouse.com
ROOMS:	4 Rooms; 1 Suite; Private and shared baths
CHILDREN:	Welcome
ANIMALS:	Not allowed
HANDICAPPED:	Not handicapped accessible
DIETARY NEEDS:	Will accommodate guests' special dietary needs

Cornmeal Yeast Waffles

Makes 6 to 10 Waffles

Plan ahead! For a special waffle treat in the morning, you must start making the batter the night before.

2	cups milk
1	package (2¼ teaspoons) active dry yeast
½	cup warm water (105-115°F)
⅓	cup butter or margarine, melted
1	teaspoon salt
1	tablespoon sugar
2	cups flour
1	cup yellow corn meal
2	large eggs, slightly beaten
½	teaspoon baking soda

In a medium saucepan, scald milk and set aside. Cool milk to lukewarm (105-115°F). In a very large bowl, sprinkle yeast into warm water. Stir until yeast is dissolved. Add lukewarm milk, butter, salt, sugar, flour and corn meal. Mix until batter is smooth. Cover and let stand at room temperature overnight. (Note: Depending on overnight kitchen temperature, the yeast mixture may double in size. Be sure to use a bowl large enough to allow for this growth. Nobody wants to find a mess in the kitchen first thing in the morning!)

In the morning, add eggs and baking soda. Beat well. Bake waffles in a preheated, lightly greased waffle iron.

> **Carol's Corner**
> *Cooked waffles may be transferred to a 200°F oven. This will keep them crisp and hot while the rest of the waffles are baked. Everyone can eat at once, including the cook!*

DeCann House

B uilt at the turn-of-the-century, the DeCann House Bed and Breakfast
overlooks Bellingham Bay and the San Juan Islands. Located approximately one hour from both Seattle, Washington and Vancouver, British
Columbia, this restored, grand old home is decorated with family
heirlooms.

Guests enjoy a savory breakfast that features Van's special egg dishes or fruit
specialties.

INNKEEPERS:	Barbara and Van Hudson
ADDRESS:	2610 Eldridge Avenue
	Bellingham, WA 98225
TELEPHONE:	(360) 734-9172
E-MAIL:	hudson@nas.com
WEBSITE:	www.decannhouse.com
ROOMS:	2 Rooms; Both with private baths
CHILDREN:	Children age 12 and older are welcome
ANIMALS:	Not allowed
HANDICAPPED:	Not handicapped accessible
DIETARY NEEDS:	Will accommodate guests' special dietary needs

Oatmeal Waffles

Makes 8 Waffles

"This is one of several recipes passed on by friends. Our neighbor gave us this one not only because it is delicious, but because it is adapted from a cookbook of food for diabetics which means it's also good for you." - Barb and Van Hudson, DeCann House

1½   cups flour
1   cup quick-cooking oats (not instant oatmeal)
1   tablespoon baking powder
½   teaspoon cinnamon
¼   teaspoon salt (optional)
2   eggs, slightly beaten
1½   cups milk
¾   stick (6 tablespoons) butter, melted
2   tablespoons brown sugar
Peaches, fresh or home canned (optional)
Vanilla yogurt (optional)

In a large bowl, stir together flour, oats, baking powder, cinnamon and salt; set aside. In a small bowl, stir together eggs, milk, butter and brown sugar. Add wet ingredients to flour mixture; stir until well blended. Pour batter onto preheated, lightly greased waffle iron. Close lid and do not open until waffles are finished.

Serving suggestion: These oatmeal waffles are wonderful topped with peaches and vanilla yogurt.

Angelica's

Overnight guests find Angelica's Bed & Breakfast a delightful refuge, but the home is also well suited to a wide variety of corporate events and special celebrations.

"The service and attention to detail were excellent. Breakfast and snacks were delicious. We will be back again and again!" ~ Guest, Angelica's Bed & Breakfast

INNKEEPERS:	Lynette & Ted Gustafson
ADDRESS:	1321 West 9th Avenue
	Spokane, WA 99204
TELEPHONE:	(509) 624-5598
E-MAIL:	info@angelicasbb.com
WEBSITE:	www.angelicasbb.com
ROOMS:	2 Rooms; 2 Suites; All with private baths
CHILDREN:	Children age 12 and older are welcome
ANIMALS:	Not allowed; Resident cat
HANDICAPPED:	Not handicapped accessible
DIETARY NEEDS:	Will accommodate guests' special dietary needs

Belgian Waffles

Makes 12 (4-inch) Waffles

4	eggs, separated
¾	cup half & half
¾	cup light sour cream
1	stick (½ cup) unsalted butter, melted
1	teaspoon vanilla
1½	cups flour
2	teaspoons baking powder
½	teaspoon baking soda
½	teaspoon salt

In large bowl, beat egg yolks until smooth and creamy. Mix in half & half, sour cream, butter and vanilla. In a separate bowl, mix flour, baking powder, baking soda and salt. Gradually beat flour mixture into sour cream mixture.

In another bowl, beat egg whites until stiff, then gently fold into batter. Cook waffles in a prepared waffle iron until golden brown, according to directions on waffle iron. These waffles are best served immediately with your favorite topping or warm maple syrup.

Autumn Pond

The Autumn Pond Bed & Breakfast is a newer ranch home designed as a B&B. As guests enter the home, their first impression will be a comfortable rustic feel. The great room has exposed cedar beams, rough cut cedar paneling and bay windows that capture the magnificent scenery of the outdoors.

End a day of outdoor activities, shopping and dining with a relaxing soak in the Autumn Pond's outdoor hot tub.

INNKEEPERS:	John & Jennifer Lorenz
ADDRESS:	10388 Titus Road
	Leavenworth, WA 98826
TELEPHONE:	(509) 548-4482; (800) 222-9661
E-MAIL:	info@autumnpond.com
WEBSITE:	www.autumnpond.com
ROOMS:	5 Rooms; All with private baths
CHILDREN:	Children age 10 and older are welcome
ANIMALS:	Not allowed; Resident dogs
HANDICAPPED:	Not handicapped accessible
DIETARY NEEDS:	Will accommodate guests' special dietary needs

Ricotta Crêpes in Vanilla Custard

Makes 4 Servings

You can make the custard and cranberry sauce a day ahead.

Crêpes and Filling:
1¼	cups milk
1	large egg
⅔	cup flour
10	ounces ricotta cheese
5	ounces cream cheese
1	egg yolk
¼	cup sugar
½	cup dried cranberries, soaked for 30 minutes in water, then drained

Sweetened sour cream (1 cup sour cream mixed with 2 tablespoons sugar)

Vanilla Custard:
1	large egg
1	cup cream
¼	cup sugar
1	teaspoon vanilla
1	teaspoon grated lemon zest

Cranberry Sauce:
1⅓	cups cranberries
⅓	cup sugar
⅓	cup orange juice

For crêpes and filling: Blend milk, egg and flour until smooth. Let batter sit for 60 minutes. Make crêpes in buttered nonstick 10-inch pan; set aside. Beat ricotta, cream cheese, egg yolk and sugar until smooth. Fold in cranberries.

For the custard: Whisk together egg, cream and sugar in medium saucepan over medium-high heat. Stir with whisk or wooden spoon until thickened (do not let mixture boil!). Remove from heat; stir in vanilla and lemon zest.

For the cranberry sauce: Cook all ingredients in saucepan until sugar is dissolved and berries start popping.

Preheat oven to 375°F. Fill crêpes with ricotta mixture and place in a greased 13x9-inch pan. Pour custard over crêpes. Bake until set, 20-30 minutes. Serve 2 crêpes per person. Top with cranberry sauce and sweetened sour cream.

Salisbury House

Built in 1904, the Salisbury House has been an urban bed and breakfast inn since 1985. The public rooms are large and bright. A full breakfast that features luscious seasonal fruits and delectable breads and muffins is served in the sunny dining room.

The five guest rooms are each individually decorated and have private baths. Certain rooms have cushioned window seats and walk-in closets.

INNKEEPERS:	Cathryn & Mary Wiese
ADDRESS:	750 16th Avenue East
	Seattle, WA 98112
TELEPHONE:	(206) 328-8682
E-MAIL:	sleep@salisburyhouse.com
WEBSITE:	www.salisburyhouse.com
ROOMS:	5 Rooms; All with private baths
CHILDREN:	Children age 12 and older are welcome
ANIMALS:	Not allowed
HANDICAPPED:	Not handicapped accessible
DIETARY NEEDS:	Will accommodate guests' special dietary needs

Baked Blintz

Makes 8 servings

This is much easier than filling individual crêpes. It is a great recipe for entertaining a group. "Over the years this has been one of our most requested recipes. It makes a perfect brunch dish and it can be assembled the night before, refrigerated and baked in the morning." ~ Cathryn and Mary Wiese, Salisbury House

Filling:

1	(8-ounce) package cream cheese, room temperature
1	cup low-fat, small curd cottage cheese
1	egg, beaten
1	tablespoon sugar
1	teaspoon vanilla

Batter:

1	stick (½ cup) butter or margarine, room temperature
⅓	cup sugar
4	eggs
1	cup flour
2	teaspoons baking powder
1	cup plain yogurt
½	cup low-fat sour cream
½	cup orange juice

Suggested toppings: sour cream, yogurt, fresh berry preserves, fresh raspberries or cherry pie filling

To make filling: Preheat oven to 375°F. Butter and flour a 13x9-inch baking dish. In a small bowl, combine cream cheese, cottage cheese, egg, sugar and vanilla. Beat well and set aside.

To make batter: In a large bowl, cream together butter and sugar. Add eggs, one at a time; beat well after each addition. Stir in flour and baking powder. Mix in yogurt, sour cream and orange juice.

To make blintz: Pour half of batter into baking dish. Spoon filling mixture over batter, then pour remaining batter over all. Bake for 45-50 minutes, or until lightly browned. Cut into squares and serve with suggested toppings.

Chinaberry Hill

Perched on a hill overlooking Puget Sound, Chinaberry Hill is a remarkable garden retreat that works its magic on anyone who enters. Examples of unexpected whimsical combinations found throughout the house include a primitive chest surrounded with fiberglass chicken weather vanes, art deco theater curtains and a buzz-saw fishing bear.

This 1889 Victorian is on the National Register of Historic Places.

INNKEEPERS:	Cecil & Yarrow Wayman
ADDRESS:	302 Tacoma Avenue North
	North Tacoma, WA 98403
TELEPHONE:	(253) 272-1282
E-MAIL:	chinaberry@wa.net
WEBSITE:	www.chinaberryhill.com
ROOMS:	5 Suites; All with private baths
CHILDREN:	Children welcome in the guest cottage
ANIMALS:	Not allowed; Resident cats
HANDICAPPED:	Not handicapped accessible
DIETARY NEEDS:	Will accommodate guests' special dietary needs

Bernie's Zucchini-Cheddar Blintzes

Makes 10 Blintzes (Allow 1-2 per Person)

"The guest who gave us this recipe is credited in the name. Thicker than a normal blintz, they are highly aromatic, turn a golden brown and draw rave reviews whenever they are served. Best of all, they are quick, simple and extremely filling." ~ Cecil Wayman, Chinaberry Hill

1	cup baking mix (such as Krusteaz pancake mix)
1	cup milk
1	egg
1	cup grated zucchini
1	cup grated extra sharp cheddar cheese
1	teaspoon vanilla

Whipped cream cheese or vanilla yogurt
Cherry preserves or other favorite fruit preserves

Preheat a lightly oiled griddle to 350°F, or heat a lightly oiled skillet over medium-high heat. In a large bowl, using a wire whisk, combine baking mix, milk, egg, zucchini, cheddar cheese and vanilla; mix thoroughly.

Drop batter by ¼-cupfuls onto griddle (the blintzes will be about 4-inches in diameter). Turn blintzes over when edges begin to dry. Cook for about 2 minutes longer, then transfer to serving plates. Spread 1-2 tablespoons of cream cheese or yogurt on each blintz, roll up and top with preserves.

Serving suggestion: These blintzes are great with heated, thinly sliced ham. For a completely different experience, try using even more grated cheese as a filling and serve with hot spicy applesauce.

French Toast, Granola & Oatmeal

French Toast, Granola & Oatmeal

A Quail's Roost Inn

Situated on the north shore of Lake Chelan, A Quail's Roost Inn Bed and Breakfast was built in 1902 and has since been tastefully restored to its original charm. Many of the country and Victorian collectibles featured throughout this enchanting home can be purchased.

The Rose and Wicker Room features white wicker beds and hand-stenciled walls. Decorated in a French country theme, this cozy room offers a private porch and a Victorian-style bathroom.

INNKEEPERS:	Brad Stolzenburg
ADDRESS:	121 East Highland Avenue
	Chelan, WA 98816
TELEPHONE:	(509) 682-2892; (800) 681-2892
E-MAIL:	Not Available
WEBSITE:	www.aquailsroostinn.com
ROOMS:	2 Rooms; 1 Suite; All with private baths
CHILDREN:	Children age 10 and older are welcome
ANIMALS:	Not allowed
HANDICAPPED:	Not handicapped accessible
DIETARY NEEDS:	Will accommodate guests' special dietary needs

Raspberry and Cream French Toast

Makes 2 Servings

Plan ahead for this one! Soak the bread overnight or for at least several hours before cooking. "We have been serving this French toast for eight years. People return year after year asking for their favorite fruit flavor." ~ Innkeeper, A Quail's Roost Inn

3	large eggs
¾	cup half & half
6	(½-inch thick) slices French bread
1	stick (½ cup) butter, melted
½	cup frozen freezer raspberry jam, or any other favorite flavor (recipe for freezer jam can be found inside box of liquid fruit pectin)
2	tablespoons butter, for griddle

Powdered sugar, for garnish
Fresh fruit, for garnish

In a small bowl, combine eggs and half & half; mix well. Place bread slices in an ungreased 11x7-inch baking dish. Pour egg mixture evenly over bread. Cover and refrigerate for several hours or overnight, until liquid is absorbed.

Make a sauce by mixing melted butter and jam in a small bowl until well combined. Set aside until ready to serve. (The sauce can be prepared in advance and refrigerated.)

Preheat griddle to 350°F (or a skillet to medium-high). Melt 2 tablespoons butter on griddle and cook bread slices for approximately 8 minutes on each side. Warm the sauce, stirring well. Serve French toast with a drizzling of the sauce and a sprinkling of powdered sugar. Garnish with fresh fruit on top.

Caswell's on the Bay

Privacy is a main feature of Caswell's on the Bay Bed and Breakfast Inn. The guest rooms are decorated with antiques and have either a water or garden view. The finest Caswell-Massey bath amenities are provided.

"Good birding! Good relaxing! Great weekend!" ~ Guest, Caswell's on the Bay

INNKEEPERS:	Bob & Marilyn Caswell
ADDRESS:	25204 Sandridge Road
	Ocean Park, WA 98640
TELEPHONE:	(360) 665-6535; (888) 553-2319
E-MAIL:	bcaswell@willapabay.org
WEBSITE:	www.caswellsinn.com
ROOMS:	5 Rooms; All with private baths
CHILDREN:	Children age 12 and older are welcome
ANIMALS:	Not allowed
HANDICAPPED:	Not handicapped accessible
DIETARY NEEDS:	Will accommodate guests' special dietary needs

Baked Orange Pecan French Toast

Makes 4 to 6 Servings

A great make-ahead recipe. Soak the bread in an orange flavored egg batter the night before and pop it in the oven in the morning. Easy, yet elegant!

6	eggs
⅔	cup orange juice
⅓	cup milk
3	tablespoons orange liqueur
¼	cup sugar
1	tablespoon grated orange zest
½	teaspoon vanilla
¼	teaspoon nutmeg
12	thick slices French bread
⅓	cup butter, melted
½	cup chopped pecans

Powdered sugar, for garnish
Fresh fruit, for garnish
Syrup

In a large bowl, whisk or beat together eggs, orange juice, milk, orange liqueur, sugar, orange zest, vanilla and nutmeg. Dip each slice of French bread in mixture, turning to coat both sides. Place soaked bread slices in a single layer on an ungreased 15x10-inch jelly-roll pan. Pour any remaining mixture over bread. Cover with plastic wrap and refrigerate overnight.

Next morning: Preheat oven to 375°F. Divide melted butter evenly between two 13x9-inch glass baking dishes and spread to completely cover bottom of dishes. Place soaked bread slices in a single layer in the two dishes and sprinkle with pecans.

Bake on middle rack in oven for 20 minutes. Do not turn slices over. If crisper French toast is desired, raise oven temperature to 400°F and bake for 10 minutes longer, or until crisp and golden brown. Remove from baking dishes to warm plates. Sprinkle with powdered sugar and garnish with fresh fruit. Serve with a variety of syrups.

Harbor Hill Inn

Charm and comfort await guests of the Harbor Hill Inn Bed and Breakfast. This 1908 manor house was built by one of Everett's pioneer lumber mill owners. The Captain's Room has ship paintings, fishing items, collectibles and oriental rugs. The Sewing Room features old sewing machines, patchwork quilts and handmade crafts.

The nearby Everett marina offers charter salmon fishing and harbor and San Juan Island tours.

INNKEEPERS:	Paul and Mary Ehrlich
ADDRESS:	2208 Rucker Avenue
	Everett, WA 98201
TELEPHONE:	(425) 259-3925; (888) 572-3925
E-MAIL:	innkeeper@harborhillinn.com
WEBSITE:	www.harborhillinn.com
ROOMS:	5 Rooms; All with private baths
CHILDREN:	Call ahead
ANIMALS:	Not allowed
HANDICAPPED:	Not handicapped accessible
DIETARY NEEDS:	Will accommodate guests' special dietary needs

Creamy Sunshine French Toast

Makes 8 Servings

You can make the filling and batter for this French toast the night before and refrigerate both. In the morning, just spread the filling and cook the French toast. "Our guests enjoy the creamy citrus flavor and the different bread choice of this French toast. This is an excellent recipe for those mornings when guests have different time schedules. It can be prepared quickly and served fresh each time. The ingredients can be kept on-hand for drop-in guests, and makes a wonderful presentation." ~ Mary Ehrlich, Harbor Hill Inn

1	(8-ounce) package cream cheese, room temperature
¾	cup orange marmalade
4	eggs
¾	cup milk
¼	cup half & half
1	tablespoon orange liqueur (or orange extract)
1	tablespoon sugar
¼	teaspoon nutmeg
16	slices cinnamon raisin bread

Butter or oil (to grease pan)
Powdered sugar, orange slices and mint, for garnish

In a small bowl, gently mix cream cheese and marmalade; set filling aside. In a medium bowl, beat eggs, milk, half & half, orange liqueur, sugar and nutmeg; set batter aside.

To make French toast "sandwiches": Spread a small amount of filling on 8 slices of raisin bread. Top with remaining slices of bread. Heat greased skillet over medium heat. Dip each sandwich lightly in batter 1 or 2 times, coating each side. Cook sandwiches, turning 3 or 4 times to brown both sides, but keeping the filling from melting.

To serve: Slice French toast in halves or quarters, sprinkle with powdered sugar and garnish with orange slices and fresh mint.

Chambered Nautilus

Breakfast at the Chambered Nautilus Bed and Breakfast Inn is an elegant event in the antique-furnished dining room, complete with its own fireplace. Guests are treated to fresh fruit, juice, granola, baked goods and mouth-watering entrées such as Northwest Salmon Breakfast Pie or Stuffed French Toast with Homemade Orange Syrup.

Well-maintained trails and parks are nearby for walkers, joggers and bicyclists.

INNKEEPERS:	Joyce Schulte & Steven Poole
ADDRESS:	5005 22nd Avenue NE
	Seattle, WA 98105
TELEPHONE:	(206) 522-2536; (800) 545-8459
E-MAIL:	stay@chamberednautilus.com
WEBSITE:	www.chamberednautilus.com
ROOMS:	10 Rooms; 4 Suites; All with private baths
CHILDREN:	Call ahead
ANIMALS:	Not allowed
HANDICAPPED:	Not handicapped accessible
DIETARY NEEDS:	Will accommodate guests' special dietary needs

Stuffed French Toast with Orange Syrup

Makes 4 Servings

8	(1-inch thick) slices French bread
4	ounces cream cheese, room temperature
¼	cup orange marmalade
3	eggs
¾	cup milk
¼	teaspoon vanilla
⅛	teaspoon cinnamon

Dash nutmeg

2	tablespoons butter or margarine

Powdered sugar and orange slices, for garnish

Orange syrup (recipe follows)

With the point of a sharp knife, in each slice of bread, make a slit in the center of the top crust, cutting down a couple inches to make a "pocket." In a small bowl, stir cream cheese and marmalade just until combined (overstirring causes mixture to become soupy). Spoon about 1 tablespoon of cream cheese mixture into each bread pocket.

In a medium bowl, beat together eggs, milk, vanilla, cinnamon and nutmeg. Dip stuffed bread slices into egg mixture. Melt butter on griddle or in a skillet over medium heat. Cook stuffed bread slices, turning once, until golden brown on both sides. Sprinkle with powdered sugar, garnish with an orange slice and serve with orange syrup.

Orange syrup:

1	cup sugar
2	sticks (1 cup) butter
1	(6-ounce) can frozen orange juice concentrate

In a small saucepan, heat all ingredients over low heat until butter and frozen orange juice are melted (do not boil). Remove from heat and cool for 5-10 minutes. Beat until slightly thickened. Serve warm.

Tudor Inn

The Tudor Inn has been tastefully restored to retain the rustic charm of the Tudor Era, enhanced with many fine antiques from Europe and modernized to provide the comfort and ease of the present. The Inn has five guestrooms located on the second floor, all with private baths, views of the Olympic Mountains or the Strait of Juan de Fuca.

A John Broadwood grand piano from London awaits the gentle touch of guests who enjoy music.

INNKEEPERS:	Betsy Reed-Schultz
ADDRESS:	1108 South Oak Street
	Port Angeles, WA 98362
TELEPHONE:	(360) 452-3138
E-MAIL:	info@tudorinn.com
WEBSITE:	www.tudorinn.com
ROOMS:	5 Rooms; All with private baths
CHILDREN:	Children age 12 and older are welcome
ANIMALS:	Not allowed
HANDICAPPED:	Not handicapped accessible
DIETARY NEEDS:	Will accommodate guests' special dietary needs

Tudor Inn Apple French Toast

Makes 6 to 8 Servings

Caramel apple lovers will enjoy the great flavor of this French toast! Preparation is done the night before, making the morning a breeze.

1   cup plus 2 tablespoons brown sugar
1   stick (½ cup) butter
2   tablespoons light corn syrup
2   apples, peeled and thinly sliced
1   loaf French bread, sliced ¾-inch thick
5   eggs
1½   cups milk
1   teaspoon vanilla
Maple syrup

In a medium saucepan, over medium heat, combine brown sugar, butter and corn syrup. Cook, stirring frequently, until mixture starts to bubble. Remove from heat and pour into a 17x11-inch jelly-roll pan. Spread apple slices over syrup mixture in pan. Place bread slices on top of apples.

In a medium bowl, whisk or beat together eggs, milk and vanilla; pour (or spoon) mixture evenly over bread. Cover and refrigerate overnight.

Next morning: Preheat oven to 350°F. Bake French toast, uncovered, for 40-45 minutes, or until browned. Serve with maple syrup.

The Villa

THE VILLA

Upstairs at The Villa Bed and Breakfast are four unique suites, each with the amenities found in the finest hotels. The Bay View Suite offers sweeping vistas of Commencement Bay and the Olympic Mountains. The Garden Suite affords a commanding view of the Sunken Garden. The Rice Bed Suite is named for its richly carved, four-poster bed.

Tucked away on the top floor, the Maids' Quarters Suite has a private verandah.

INNKEEPERS:	Greg & Becky Anglemyer
ADDRESS:	705 North 5th Street
	Tacoma, WA 98403
TELEPHONE:	(253) 572-1157; (888) 572-1157
E-MAIL:	villabb@aol.com
WEBSITE:	www.tribnet.com/adv/bb/villa
ROOMS:	6 Rooms; 3 Suites; All with private baths
CHILDREN:	Children age 12 and older are welcome
ANIMALS:	Not allowed
HANDICAPPED:	Is handicapped accessible
DIETARY NEEDS:	Will accommodate guests' special dietary needs

Baked French Toast Cockaigne

Makes 4 Servings

Becky, at The Villa, suggests making your morning easier by preparing the topping ahead of time. The bread can even be dipped in the egg mixture the night before, arranged in individual baking dishes and refrigerated. She says it's best to add the toppings, however, just before baking.

4	eggs
1	cup milk
½	teaspoon salt
½	teaspoon vanilla
¼	cup flour
¼	cup brown sugar
¼	teaspoon cinnamon
1	tablespoon butter

8-12 (¾-inch thick) slices Italian or French bread
Cherry, blueberry or apple pie filling

Preheat oven to 400°F. In a medium bowl, combine eggs, milk, salt and vanilla; set aside. Make the topping by combining, in a small bowl, the flour, brown sugar, cinnamon and butter. Mix until crumbly; set aside.

Coat 4 individual baking dishes with nonstick cooking spray. Dip bread slices into egg/milk mixture and arrange 2-3 overlapping slices in each baking dish (the number of slices used depends on the size of the dishes as well as the size of the loaf of bread). Spread pie filling in a line across center of overlapping bread slices. Sprinkle with topping. Bake for about 15 minutes, or until browned and crispy.

> **Carol's Corner**
> *I tested this recipe using cherry pie filling. It was easy to make, colorful to serve and tasted great!*

The Inn at Burg's Landing

The logo for The Inn at Burg's Landing consists of a silhouette of two majestic evergreens that were planted in 1929 by Chester and Edna Burg in celebration of their wedding day. These trees represent the inn's steadfast commitment to the Burg family's heritage of warm, friendly and personal hospitality toward all guests who share this island refuge.

Guests enjoy spectacular views of Mount Rainier, the Cascades and Puget Sound.

INNKEEPERS:	Ken & Annie Burg
ADDRESS:	8808 Villa Beach Road
	Anderson Island, WA 98303
TELEPHONE:	(253) 884-9185; (800) 431-5622
E-MAIL:	innatburgslanding@mailexcite.com
WEBSITE:	www.burgslandingbb.com
ROOMS:	4 Rooms; Private and shared baths
CHILDREN:	Welcome
ANIMALS:	Not allowed
HANDICAPPED:	Not handicapped accessible
DIETARY NEEDS:	Will accommodate guests' special dietary needs

Baked Stuffed French Toast

Makes 4 to 5 Servings

1   (8-ounce) package cream cheese, room temperature
2   tablespoons vanilla
2   tablespoons sugar
⅓   cup chopped nuts
10 (1-inch thick) slices French bread
6   eggs
½   cup milk
½   teaspoon cinnamon
½   teaspoon nutmeg

Preheat oven to 375°F. In a small bowl, blend cream cheese, vanilla, sugar and nuts; set aside. With the point of a sharp knife, in each slice of bread, make a slit in the center of the top crust, cutting down a couple inches to make a "pocket." Spread about 1 tablespoon of cream cheese mixture in each pocket.

In a large bowl, beat together eggs, milk, cinnamon and nutmeg. Dip each slice of bread into egg mixture, soaking thoroughly. Put slices onto a greased baking sheet and bake for about 20 minutes, or until lightly browned.

Marianna Stoltz House

The decor of the Marianna Stoltz House is historically tasteful, graced throughout with beautiful antiques. Each of the four guest chambers in this Historic Landmark house are appointed with a different color scheme with hints of the 1908 era in which the house was constructed.

Ivy and white take over the Ivy Suite, with large private bath and clawfoot soaking tub for two. Antique oak dresser and a rocking chair make this a perfect place for honeymoons, anniversaries or just a quiet night away.

INNKEEPERS:	Phyllis Maguire
ADDRESS:	427 East Indiana
	Spokane, WA 99207
TELEPHONE:	(509) 483-4316; (800) 978-6587
E-MAIL:	info@mariannastoltzhouse.com
WEBSITE:	www.mariannastoltzhouse.com
ROOMS:	4 Rooms; 1 Suite; Private and shared baths
CHILDREN:	Welcome
ANIMALS:	Not allowed
HANDICAPPED:	Not handicapped accessible
DIETARY NEEDS:	Will accommodate guests' special dietary needs

Stoltz House Special French Toast

Makes 4 Servings

This is a delicious French toast that is very easy to make. The French toast needs to soak overnight.

6   (diagonally cut, ¾-inch thick) slices French bread
3   eggs
1   cup light cream
2   tablespoons orange marmalade
½   teaspoon nutmeg
1½   tablespoons butter
1½   tablespoons vegetable oil
Powdered sugar
Mandarin strawberry topping (recipe follows)

Arrange bread in single layer in a baking pan. Combine eggs, cream, preserves and nutmeg. Beat until smooth and pour over bread. Turn slices to coat evenly. Cover and refrigerate overnight.

To cook, heat butter and oil in pan. Cook bread slices in butter and oil until golden brown, about 5 minutes on each side. Top with powdered sugar and hot mandarin strawberry topping.

Mandarin strawberry topping:
1   (11-ounce) can mandarin oranges
1   (10-ounce) package frozen strawberry halves, thawed
Water, as needed
2   tablespoons sugar
1   tablespoon plus 1½ teaspoons cornstarch
1   teaspoon lemon juice

Drain orange segments and strawberries, reserving juice from both. Add enough water to reserved juice to make 1½ cups of liquid. Combine sugar, cornstarch and juice mixture in a medium saucepan. Bring to a boil over medium-high heat. Stirring constantly, boil and stir for 1 minute. Stir in lemon juice, orange segments and strawberries. Serve hot.

Island Escape

Guests of the Island Escape Bed and Breakfast enjoy a luxurious first floor suite furnished with a beautifully carved German hutch, California King-size bed and private Jacuzzi bath. Innkeeper Paula Pascoe offers additional amenities in the popular "Honeymoon Package."

"We came for one night and stayed for four. This is the finest place we've ever stayed." ~ Guest, Island Escape

INNKEEPERS:	Paula E. Pascoe
ADDRESS:	210 Island Boulevard
	Fox Island, WA 98333
TELEPHONE:	(253) 549-2044; (877) 549-2044
E-MAIL:	paula@island-escape.com
WEBSITE:	www.island-escape.com
ROOMS:	1 Executive Suite; Private bath
CHILDREN:	Welcome
ANIMALS:	Call ahead
HANDICAPPED:	Not handicapped accessible
DIETARY NEEDS:	Will accommodate guests' special dietary needs

Island Escape's House Granola

Makes About 8 Cups

"Credit for this recipe goes to Kim, my husband's daughter. She was a blue ribbon graduate of Peter Kump's New York Cooking School and is currently a Pastry Assistant at The Coyote Café in Santa Fe. Several of Kim's recipes are incorporated in our menus at Island Escape. We serve this House Granola with our hot Montana whole-wheat cereal. It is the main entrée and is presented with a seasonal fresh fruit plate and homemade muffins or a quick bread. You can easily add your own touches to this delicious granola. For a distinctive 'island' flavor, add coconut and dried, unsweetened pineapple. Or add your favorite dried fruits, such as apricots, apples, banana chips and cranberries or craisins." ~ Paula Pascoe, Island Escape

4	cups rolled oats
¼	cup unrefined safflower oil
¼	cup honey
1½	teaspoons vanilla
½	cup sesame seeds
½	cup chopped unsalted almonds
½	cup chopped unsalted cashews
1	cup raisins

Preheat oven to 350°F. Using a very large cookie sheet or large shallow baking pan, toast rolled oats in oven for 15 minutes, stirring once or twice to ensure even baking.

In a small saucepan, combine oil, honey and vanilla. Heat until warm, then set aside. In a large bowl, combine sesame seeds, almonds and cashews. Pour the warm oil/honey mixture over seeds and nuts. Stir to combine and then pour combined mixture over the oats. Blend well.

Bake for about 20 minutes, turning oats every 5 minutes. Watch carefully so the granola mixture doesn't get too browned. Add raisins and any other desired ingredients when the granola is done baking.

The James House

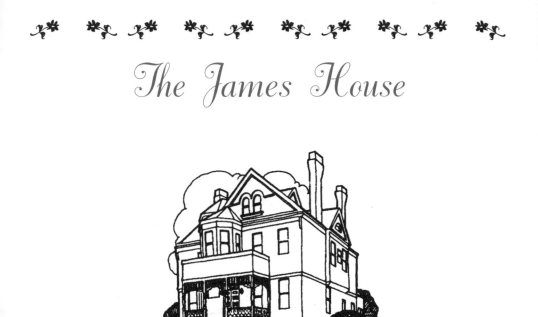

Sitting high on a bluff overlooking Port Townsend Bay, The James House is a grand Victorian mansion with sweeping views of the Cascade and Olympic mountain ranges. On the National Register of Historic Places, this stately mansion is a reminder of a bygone era when the bay was filled with sailing ships.

The James House was the first bed and breakfast in the Pacific Northwest.

INNKEEPERS:	Carol McGough
ADDRESS:	1238 Washington Street
	Port Townsend, WA 98368
TELEPHONE:	(360) 385-1238; (800) 385-1238
E-MAIL:	carolmcg@olympus.net
WEBSITE:	www.jameshouse.com
ROOMS:	8 Rooms; 4 Suites; 1 Cottage; All with private baths
CHILDREN:	Children age 12 and older are welcome
ANIMALS:	Not allowed
HANDICAPPED:	Not handicapped accessible
DIETARY NEEDS:	Will accommodate guests' special dietary needs

Fruit and Yogurt Bircher Muesli

Makes 12 Servings

2   cups rolled oats
Milk (enough to cover oats)
¾   cup seedless red grapes
1   cup pineapple, diced (fresh or canned)
2   pears, diced (fresh or canned)
½   banana, halved and sliced
16   ounces peach yogurt
⅓   cup honey, warmed slightly (aids mixing)
2   sweet apples
1   cup coconut, more or less to taste, toasted (directions follow)

Place uncooked oats in a medium bowl and add enough milk to just cover
the oats. Let stand for 15 minutes. Meanwhile, in a large bowl, combine
grapes, pineapple, pears and banana. Stir in the yogurt; set aside. Add
honey to oats, mixing well. Grate apples (peeled or unpeeled) and mix into
oats. Add oat/apple mixture to fruit/yogurt mixture. Serve ½-cup portions
in individual bowls and top each with 1 tablespoon toasted coconut.

For toasted coconut: Preheat oven to 350°F. Spread coconut in a single
layer on a cookie sheet or in a shallow baking pan. Bake for about 10
minutes, stirring occasionally, until coconut is evenly browned and lightly
toasted (be careful not to overcook it – it will burn easily). Cool completely
and store in airtight container.

Carol's Corner

*The German word muesli means mixture. Muesli was
developed as a health food at the end of the 19th century
by a Swiss nutritionist named Dr. Bircher-Benner.
Muesli is a delicious and healthful way to start the day.*

Egg Entrées & Breakfast Dishes

Egg Dishes & Breakfast Entrées

Baker House

S crumptious, three-course breakfasts await guests of the Baker House Bed and Breakfast. Located three blocks from the waterfront, this historic inn affords gorgeous views of Port Townsend Bay.

"This is what a B&B should be like." ~ Guest, Baker House B&B

INNKEEPERS:	Herb & Jean Herrington
ADDRESS:	905 Franklin
	Port Townsend, WA 98368
TELEPHONE:	(360) 385-6673
E-MAIL:	hnjherrington@olympus.net
WEBSITE:	Not available
ROOMS:	4 Rooms; Private and shared baths
CHILDREN:	Children age 14 and older are welcome
ANIMALS:	Not allowed
HANDICAPPED:	Not handicapped accessible
DIETARY NEEDS:	Will accommodate guests' special dietary needs

Herb's Special Breakfast

Makes 2 to 4 Servings (Depending on Size of Appetites)

"You can modify this recipe to be a light dinner meal. Instead of the ground beef, substitute any combination of shelled shrimp, scallops and white fish, only add them just before the eggs so they don't get overcooked." ~ Herb Herrington, Baker House

1	tablespoon oil
2	cups chopped onion (Herb likes up to 3 cups)
1-2	cloves garlic, minced
½	pound lean ground beef

Salt and pepper, to taste
Oregano, to taste

1	(8-ounce) can sliced mushrooms, drained
⅓	(10-ounce) package frozen chopped spinach, thawed
4	eggs, well beaten
¼	cup grated Parmesan cheese

Heat oil in a large skillet. Cook onions until just softened. Add garlic and cook a few minutes more. Stir in beef and cook until meat is done but still a little pink in places. Season with salt, pepper and oregano. Drain off fat, if any. (Note: At this point the pan may be covered and set aside as you prepare the rest of your meal.)

To finish the dish: Squeeze out moisture from spinach. Add spinach and mushrooms to meat mixture and heat through. Adjust seasonings, if needed. Add the eggs. Cook until eggs are fully cooked (mixture will be fairly dry). Serve on warmed plates and sprinkle with Parmesan cheese.

Serving suggestion: Toast and sliced fresh fruit go well with this dish.

Olympic Lights

Overlooking the panorama of the Pacific Ocean and the Olympic Mountain Range, the Olympic Lights Bed and Breakfast sits in an open meadow on San Juan Island. Guests of this wondrous guest home recapture simple pleasures by walking through open meadows and strolling the spectacular beaches of American Camp.

A full breakfast includes eggs from the resident hens.

INNKEEPERS:	Christian & Lea Andrade
ADDRESS:	146 Starlight Way
	Friday Harbor, WA 98250
TELEPHONE:	(360) 378-3186; (888) 211-6195
E-MAIL:	christian-lea@olympiclights.com
WEBSITE:	www.olympiclights.com
ROOMS:	4 Rooms; All with private baths
CHILDREN:	Children age 10 and older are welcome
ANIMALS:	Not allowed
HANDICAPPED:	Not handicapped accessible
DIETARY NEEDS:	Call ahead

Eggs and Potatoes with Red Pepper-Onion Sauce

Makes 6 Servings

Make the red pepper-onion sauce ahead of time. Freeze in small one-cup portions and you'll be ready to make this egg dish almost any time. This is a great breakfast dish, and a perfect one for vegetarians!

2	tablespoons olive oil or butter
1	cup chopped sweet onion
2	cups (¼-inch) cubes cooked red potato
1	cup Red Pepper-Onion Sauce (recipe follows)
12	eggs, beaten
2	tablespoons cottage cheese
¾	cup grated cheddar cheese

Heat olive oil or butter in skillet and cook onion until tender. Add potatoes and 1 cup of Red Pepper-Onion Sauce. Heat through and then set aside; cover with foil to keep warm. In a large nonstick pan, coated with cooking spray or butter, cook eggs over very low heat. Just as eggs begin to set, add cottage cheese. Remove from heat (eggs should be very moist). Coat 6 individual baking dishes with nonstick cooking spray. Spoon eggs into dishes and top with potato mixture. Sprinkle each dish with 2 tablespoons cheddar cheese. Broil for about 3 minutes and serve.

Red Pepper-Onion Sauce:
2-3 red bell peppers
¾ large sweet white onion, chopped
Salt, to taste

Cut peppers lengthwise, remove seeds and stems. Place peppers skin-side up on a foil-covered cookie sheet. Broil for about 10 minutes, until skin is charred. Seal peppers in a brown paper bag for about 15 minutes. Peel skin. Cook chopped onions in olive oil or butter until caramelized. Purée onions and peppers in food processor or blender. Add salt, if desired. Freeze extra sauce for later use.

Marianna Stoltz House

The Marianna Stoltz House has been a peaceful haven for travelers and visiting professionals since 1987. The bed and breakfast is close to downtown Spokane for easy access to the Convention Center, Opera House, Ag Center, the Arena and shopping areas.

The view of fresh snow on the huge spruce trees greets every window in the Blue Room in winter. In summer, the same windows embrace you in sunshine and elegant lace.

INNKEEPERS:	Phyllis Maguire
ADDRESS:	427 East Indiana
	Spokane, WA 99207
TELEPHONE:	(509) 483-4316; (800) 978-6587
E-MAIL:	info@mariannastoltzhouse.com
WEBSITE:	www.mariannastoltzhouse.com
ROOMS:	4 Rooms; 1 Suite; Private and shared baths
CHILDREN:	Children are welcome
ANIMALS:	Not allowed
HANDICAPPED:	Not handicapped accessible
DIETARY NEEDS:	Will accommodate guests' special dietary needs

Sunday Morning Eggs

Makes 4 Servings

This is a favorite! It's very simple and can be multiplied or divided to fit any number of guests. If you don't have individual ramekins, you can use custard cups or small soufflé dishes. Or you can use a large casserole dish and divide the eggs at serving time. Serve it with fruit, toast and homemade jam.

2	tablespoons butter or margarine
¼	cup finely chopped onion
1	cup sliced mushrooms
½	cup cubed cooked ham
1	cup sour cream
¼	teaspoon white pepper
2	teaspoons minced fresh dill or 1 teaspoon dried dill weed
8	eggs
4	tablespoons freshly grated Parmesan cheese

Preheat oven to 500°F. In a large skillet over medium heat, melt the butter. Add the onion, mushrooms and ham; cook until onion is soft. Divide mushroom mixture among 4 greased ramekins or small casserole dishes.

In a small bowl, combine sour cream, ground pepper and dill. Divide mixture among the ramekins, then smooth it in a circle to create a depression in the middle of each dish. Break 2 eggs into each depression, making sure that the eggs to do not touch the edges of the dish (or they will cook unevenly). Top each dish with 1 tablespoon of Parmesan cheese. Bake until eggs are set, about 7-10 minutes.

Kangaroo House

Kangaroo House Bed & Breakfast is a stately old Craftsman-style home, built in 1907 by D.W. Gafford. In the early 1930s, Captain Harold (Cap) Ferris purchased the home. In 1953, Cap brought a kangaroo named Josie home from a voyage to Australia. Josie delighted Cap's family and islanders with her antics. She was also adept at predicting the weather – everyone knew a storm was brewing when Josie chose to spend the night under the big cedar tree. The islanders and their children loved Josie and this lovely old home has been known as "Kangaroo House" ever since.

INNKEEPERS:	Peter & Helen Allen
ADDRESS:	1459 North Beach Road, PO Box 334
	Eastsound, WA 98245
TELEPHONE:	(360) 376-2175; (888) 371-2175
E-MAIL:	innkeeper@kangaroohouse.com
WEBSITE:	www.kangaroohouse.com
ROOMS:	4 Rooms; 1 Suite; Private and shared baths
CHILDREN:	Welcome
ANIMALS:	Not allowed
HANDICAPPED:	Not handicapped accessible
DIETARY NEEDS:	Will accommodate guests' special dietary needs

Portobello Breakfast Caps

Makes 2 Servings

Jones Dairy Farm invited more than 2,400 inns to create new recipes using Jones Farm meat products and submit them in a nation-wide contest. Helen won First Prize in the Northwest Region for these Portobello Breakfast Caps.

1	medium red bell pepper, roasted, peeled and halved
2	medium (about 5-inches in diameter) portobello mushrooms
6	leaves fresh spinach, washed
4	ounces Jones All-Natural Roll Sausage, or other bulk sausage
4	large eggs
1	dash Tabasco sauce

Salt and pepper, to taste

1	tablespoon snipped fresh chives
1	teaspoon butter
½	cup grated cheddar cheese, divided
2	tablespoons grated Parmesan cheese

Fresh, vine-ripened tomato slices and fresh herbs, for garnish

Preheat oven to 350°F. Remove stems and gills from mushrooms. Place prepared mushroom caps on baking sheet and roast in oven for approximately 20 minutes.

Meanwhile, briefly steam spinach just to wilt, or microwave for about 1 minute; set aside. Cook sausage until brown. Drain and set aside. In a small bowl, whisk together eggs, Tabasco, salt, pepper and chives. In a non-stick skillet, melt butter, then add egg mixture and scramble to moist scramble stage. Add browned sausage and ¼ cup grated cheddar cheese; combine just to melt cheese (avoid letting eggs get too dry).

To assemble: Line each mushroom cap with a layer of wilted spinach leaves, then a layer of roasted red pepper. Divide scrambled egg/sausage mixture atop the mushrooms. Sprinkle with Parmesan and remaining ¼ cup cheddar cheese. Place in oven until cheese is melted, about 1-2 minutes.

To serve: With a serrated knife, slice each mushroom cap in half and separate slightly to display layers. Garnish with tomato slices and herbs.

Soundview

Located 100 feet above Puget Sound, the Soundview Bed and Breakfast is a solitary guest house that overlooks the shipping lanes between Seattle and Tacoma. This private suite includes a kitchen, dining area, living room and bedroom with king-sized bed. A delectable breakfast is served after a peaceful night's rest.

From the deck, guests enjoy glorious sunsets while observing the resident eagles.

INNKEEPERS:	Sari Spieler & Daniel Goldsmith
ADDRESS:	17600 Sylvester Road SW
	Seattle, WA 98166
TELEPHONE:	(206) 244-5209; (888) 244-5209
E-MAIL:	soundview@soundviewbnb.com
WEBSITE:	www.soundviewbandb.com
ROOMS:	1 Cottage; Private bath
CHILDREN:	Not allowed
ANIMALS:	Not allowed
HANDICAPPED:	Is handicapped accessible
DIETARY NEEDS:	Will accommodate guests' special dietary needs

Baked Egg and Potato Puff

Makes 2 Servings

4	eggs
2	teaspoons water
¼	cup grated cheddar cheese
8	mini Tater Tots (or use 4 regular size and cut in half)

Preheat oven to 350°F. Coat two (1-cup) ramekins with nonstick cooking spray. In a medium bowl, beat together eggs and water. Add cheese and potatoes. Stir to combine. Divide between two ramekins. Bake uncovered for 20-25 minutes – it will puff up like a soufflé. Serve immediately.

Make-ahead tip: After baking, these can be cooled, covered with plastic wrap and refrigerated. Reheat in microwave.

Carol's Corner

I tried this recipe using a ¾-cup ramekin. The uncooked egg mixture filled the dish to the very top. After 25 minutes of baking, the egg and potato had puffed up to 1½-inches above the rim of the dish. It looked great to serve! I suggest offering ketchup or salsa for those who like the extra flavor.

Fotheringham House

Mornings at The Fotheringham House begin with the inn's own blend of coffee or tea, placed outside your bedroom door, followed by a full breakfast in the dining room.

"Nearly 55 varieties of old garden roses, many from mid-19th-century plants, are the highlight here. Roses peak in mid June, but the gardens sprout color from daffodils and cherry trees in springtime and maples in the fall." ~ *Sunset* magazine, February, 2000

INNKEEPERS:	Poul & Irene Jensen
ADDRESS:	2128 West Second Avenue
	Spokane, WA 99204
TELEPHONE:	(509) 838-1891
E-MAIL:	innkeeper@fotheringham.net
WEBSITE:	www.fotheringham.net
ROOMS:	3 Rooms; Private and shared baths
CHILDREN:	Children age 12 and older are welcome
ANIMALS:	Not allowed
HANDICAPPED:	Not handicapped accessible
DIETARY NEEDS:	Will accommodate guests' special dietary needs

Turkey Sausage & Egg Bake

Makes 10 to 12 Servings

1	pound bulk turkey breakfast sausage or turkey Italian sausage
1	tablespoon butter or oil
2	cups sliced mushrooms
5	green onions, sliced
¼	red bell pepper, diced
2	tablespoons finely chopped rosemary
12	eggs, beaten
1	(10-ounce) can cream of mushroom soup
1	cup milk

Salt and pepper, to taste

1   cup grated sharp cheddar cheese

Preheat oven to 350°F. Brown and crumble turkey sausage. Drain well and place in 9x13-inch pan. Heat butter or oil in a skillet. Add mushrooms, green onions, red bell pepper and rosemary; cook until crisp-tender. Drain well and add to cooked sausage.

Combine beaten eggs, soup, milk, salt and pepper; add to sausage mixture. Cover with cheddar cheese. Bake for 40-45 minutes.

Fotheringham House

The Fotheringham House Bed and Breakfast is a Queen Anne Victorian home constructed in 1891 by David B. Fotheringham, Spokane's first mayor. Decorated with period European and mid-Victorian American walnut furniture, this historic home retains much of its original charm.

Most of the window glass, the intricate ball and spindle fretwork in the foyer, and the open staircase are features from the original home.

INNKEEPERS:	Poul and Irene Jensen
ADDRESS:	2128 West Second Avenue
	Spokane, WA 99204
TELEPHONE:	(509) 838-1891
E-MAIL:	innkeeper@fotheringham.net
WEBSITE:	www.fotheringham.net
ROOMS:	3 Rooms; Private and shared baths
CHILDREN:	Children age 12 and older are welcome
ANIMALS:	Not allowed
HANDICAPPED:	Not handicapped accessible
DIETARY NEEDS:	Will accommodate guests' special dietary needs

Easy Eggs Benedict

Makes 4 Servings

A no-fail Hollandaise sauce, quick and easy to prepare. It is very flavorful and has a smooth, creamy consistency.

1   stick (½ cup) butter
3   egg yolks
2   tablespoons lemon juice
¼   teaspoon salt
Dash of white pepper
½   teaspoon prepared mustard (Dijon recommended)
4   English muffins, sliced and toasted
8   slices ham, warmed
8   eggs, poached
Paprika
Fruit to garnish (such as kiwi, strawberries or melon)

Heat butter in a small saucepan until bubbly but not browned. Put egg yolks, lemon juice, salt, white pepper and mustard in blender. Cover and run on low for about 5 seconds. While blender is running, slowly add butter until blades are covered. Blend on high for a second or two. Serve immediately on muffins that have been covered with ham and poached eggs. Sprinkle with paprika for color and garnish with fresh fruit.

Tip: Have plates ready to go, except for the Hollandaise sauce. Make the sauce last and serve immediately (do not make the sauce ahead of time or try to reheat it – it will lose its smooth consistency).

Stratford Manor

The Stratford Manor Bed and Breakfast is situated on 30 acres with panoramic views of the Pacific Northwest countryside. The rooms offer a romantic escape with their cozy comforters, sitting areas, gas fireplaces and Jacuzzi tubs.

"Thanks for the pampering." ~ Guest, Stratford Manor

INNKEEPERS:	Leslie & Jim Lohse
ADDRESS:	4566 Anderson Way
	Bellingham, WA 98226
TELEPHONE:	(360) 715-8441; (800) 240-6779
E-MAIL:	llohse@aol.com
WEBSITE:	www.stratfordmanor.com
ROOMS:	3 Rooms; All with private baths
CHILDREN:	Not allowed
ANIMALS:	Not allowed
HANDICAPPED:	Not handicapped accessible
DIETARY NEEDS:	Will accommodate guests' special dietary needs

Veggie Benedict

Makes 4 Servings

A colorful medley of vegetables teamed with poached eggs.

1-2 tablespoons olive oil
4 potatoes, diced (peeled or unpeeled)
Salt and pepper, to taste
Dried, crushed basil leaves, to taste
½ green bell pepper, thinly sliced
½ red or orange bell pepper, thinly sliced
½ yellow bell pepper, thinly sliced
¾ cup sliced mushrooms
3 green onions, sliced
Hollandaise sauce (your favorite recipe or use Knorr's mix)
4 eggs, poached
Optional garnishes: paprika, parsley, fresh fruit, edible flowers

Heat olive oil in a large skillet over medium heat. Add potatoes and season with salt, pepper and basil; cook for approximately 20 minutes. Add remaining vegetables and cook until crisp-tender. While vegetables are cooking, prepare Hollandaise sauce and cook eggs.

To serve: Divide vegetables between 4 plates. Place a poached egg on each and top with sauce. Garnish with paprika and parsley and, if desired, decorate each plate with fresh fruit and edible flowers.

The Compass Rose

The Compass Rose Bed and Breakfast on Whidbey Island, is idyllically situated in Coupeville, the heart of Ebey's Landing Historical Reserve. This elegant 1890s Queen Anne Victorian home is furnished with glorious antiques.

After arrival, guests enjoy afternoon tea. A sumptuous breakfast is presented on exquisite china, crystal, silver, linen and lace.

INNKEEPERS:	Captain & Mrs. Marshall Bronson
ADDRESS:	508 South Main Street
	Coupeville, WA 98239
TELEPHONE:	(360) 678-5318; (800) 237-3881
E-MAIL:	Not available
WEBSITE:	www.compassrosebandb.com
ROOMS:	2 Rooms; Private and shared baths
CHILDREN:	Well-behaved children are welcome
ANIMALS:	Not allowed
HANDICAPPED:	Not handicapped accessible
DIETARY NEEDS:	Will accommodate guests' special dietary needs

Wild Rice Omelets

Makes 4 Servings

4	eggs
2	tablespoons cream
½	teaspoon dried chervil (or parsley)
¼	teaspoon salt
¼	teaspoon pepper
1	tablespoon plus 4 teaspoons butter
1	small onion, chopped
½	red bell pepper, chopped
½	green bell pepper, chopped
½	yellow bell pepper, chopped
1	teaspoon herbes de Provence (or Italian seasoning)
1	cup cooked wild rice (cooked in chicken or vegetable stock)

Parsley, fresh herbs and nasturtium (edible) flowers, for garnish

In a medium bowl, beat together eggs, cream, chervil, salt and pepper until frothy. In a medium skillet, melt 1 tablespoon butter and cook onions in butter until translucent. Add the red, green and yellow bell peppers and Herbes de Provence; cook until peppers are crisp-tender.

In a 6-inch cast-iron skillet (or other ovenproof pan), over medium-low heat, melt 1 teaspoon butter. Add ¼ of the egg mixture. Over the eggs, sprinkle ¼ of the wild rice and ¼ of the sautéed vegetables. Cook for 1 minute, then place pan under broiler (2nd shelf or about 7-inches down) for about 2 minutes, until eggs set and begin to rise. Remove to warm plate and repeat to make 3 more omelets. Garnish with parsley, fresh herbs and nasturtium flowers.

> ### Carol's Corner
> There is a great spice and tea shop in Seattle's Pike Place Market called MarketSpice. They sell items in bulk, so you can buy small amounts of spices and herbs that you don't use often (like the herbes de Provence and chervil used in the above recipe). They also have a variety of salt-free seasonings and regular and flavored coffees. Stop in ... you'll enjoy the experience.

DeCann House

Located in a university town, the DeCann House Bed and Breakfast overlooks Bellingham Bay and the San Juan Islands. Innkeepers Barbara and Van are life-long Northwest residents who have restored this grand old home.

Barbara is a glass hobbyist who has decorated the house with stained glass and etchings. Van, a jack-of-all-trades, has renovated seven older homes.

INNKEEPERS:	Barbara & Van Hudson
ADDRESS:	2610 Eldridge Avenue
	Bellingham, WA 98225
TELEPHONE:	(360) 734-9172
E-MAIL:	hudson@nas.com
WEBSITE:	www.decannhouse.com
ROOMS:	2 Rooms; Both with private baths
CHILDREN:	Children age 12 and older are welcome
ANIMALS:	Not allowed
HANDICAPPED:	Not handicapped accessible
DIETARY NEEDS:	Will accommodate guests' special dietary needs

DeCann House Omelet

Makes 2 Servings (Double or Triple as Needed)

"This microwave dish has become Van's favorite breakfast to cook and serve, mainly because it is the kind of 'fill 'em up' breakfast he likes to eat. The trick is to experiment with the amount and type of cheese until you get the taste you like." ~ Barb Hudson, DeCann House

2	tablespoons butter
1	green onion, sliced
2	cups frozen hash browns

Salt and pepper, to taste

2	eggs
1	tablespoon milk
2	strips bacon, cooked and crumbled
¾	cup grated cheddar cheese
2	tablespoons cream cheese, cubed

In a 9-inch glass pie pan (or other microwave-safe dish), cook butter and onion in microwave oven for 30 seconds. Add hashbrowns, salt and pepper. Microwave on high for 2 minutes. Stir and microwave for 2 more minutes. In a small bowl, lightly beat eggs and milk. Pour over hashbrowns. Add cooked bacon; stir. Sprinkle cheddar cheese (save a bit of grated cheese for garnish) and cream cheese on top of eggs and potatoes.

Cook omelet in microwave for 2 minutes. Check edges to see if more time is needed. Eggs should be moist, but not runny (be careful not to overcook them). If more time is needed, cook for another minute and check often. Put remaining cheese on top just before serving. We usually serve these omelets with juice and toast with homemade jam.

A Touch of Europe

A Touch of Europe Bed and Breakfast Inn is a Queen Anne Victorian listed on the National Register of Historic Places. Guests awaken to an appetizing European breakfast served in the Victorian dining room or privately in the turret.

Special arrangements can be made for gourmet picnic basket lunches, elegant four to seven course dinners or catering for weddings, meetings or other special events.

INNKEEPERS:	Erika G. & James A. Cenci
ADDRESS:	220 North 16th Avenue
	Yakima, WA 98902
TELEPHONE:	(509) 454-9775; (888) 438-7073
E-MAIL:	atoeurope@msn.com
WEBSITE:	www.winesnw.com/toucheuropeb&b.htm
ROOMS:	3 Rooms; All with private baths
CHILDREN:	Not allowed
ANIMALS:	Not allowed
HANDICAPPED:	Not handicapped accessible
DIETARY NEEDS:	Will accommodate guests' special dietary needs

Signature Brie-Chives Omelet

Makes 1 Omelet

2   eggs
1   teaspoon cold water
½   tablespoon unsalted butter
½   tablespoon chopped chives
1   ounce Brie cheese, cut into ¼-inch cubes
Fresh fruit or tomato slices for garnish

In a small bowl, lightly beat together eggs and water. Melt butter in a omelet pan or skillet. Pour in eggs and scatter the chives and Brie evenly over the eggs. Make omelet swiftly, lifting cooked edges with a spatula and allowing uncooked portion of eggs to run underneath. Fold over and turn out onto a warm plate. Garnish with fresh fruit or tomato slices.

Carol's Corner

A melt-in-your-mouth omelet! This recipe is easy to do, yet has an elegant appeal. For extra garnish, slide two long chive pieces partway under the omelet.

Domaine Madeleine

Eclectic European menus are legendary at Domaine Madeleine Bed and Breakfast. Artistic arrays of fruit, fresh-baked petite baguettes and croissants are served each morning with an assortment of cheeses and jams. Appetizing breakfast entrées follow, with a light dessert being the final course of a lavish morning meal.

The five romantic guest rooms feature fireplaces and whirlpools for two.

INNKEEPERS:	Jeri Weinhold
ADDRESS:	146 Wildflower Lane
	Port Angeles, WA 98362
TELEPHONE:	(360) 457-4174; (888) 811-8376
E-MAIL:	romance@domainemadeleine.com
WEBSITE:	www.domainemadeleine.com
ROOMS:	1 Room; 3 Suites; 1 Cottage; All with private baths
CHILDREN:	Children age 12 and older are welcome
ANIMALS:	Not allowed
HANDICAPPED:	Not handicapped accessible
DIETARY NEEDS:	Will accommodate guests' special dietary needs

Madeleine's Ratatouille Omelet

Serves 2 (Makes 1 Large Omelet)

Plan ahead for this recipe. To make this flavorful omelet, you must first make Madeleine's wonderful ratatouille that is found on page 197.

2	tablespoons olive oil
4	eggs (or 3 whole eggs plus 2 egg whites), beaten
4	tablespoons ratatouille (recipe on page 197), warmed
1	tablespoon grated Emmentaler Swiss cheese
1	tablespoon grated Vermont sharp cheddar cheese

Heat oil in an omelet pan or skillet. Pour in beaten eggs. When eggs are firm, but not dry, spoon ratatouille over eggs. Fold omelet and sprinkle the grated Swiss and cheddar cheese over the top. Cut in half and serve.

All Seasons River Inn

All Seasons River Inn was built as a bed and breakfast, nestled in the evergreens of Leavenworth. It sits 80 feet above the Wenatchee River. The inn provides elegant lodging where you can relax and enjoy the breathtaking beauty of the Cascade Mountains setting.

Guests can visit Leavenworth's shops, schedule an indulgent massage, dine at one of the area's excellent restaurants, take a carriage ride or enjoy stellar musical events.

INNKEEPERS:	Kathy & Jeff Falconer
ADDRESS:	8751 Icicle Road
	Leavenworth, WA 98826
TELEPHONE:	(509) 548-1425; (800) 254-0555
E-MAIL:	info@allseasonsriverinn.com
WEBSITE:	www.allseasonsriverinn.com
ROOMS:	6 Rooms; 3 Suites; All with private baths
CHILDREN:	Children age 16 and older are welcome
ANIMALS:	Not allowed
HANDICAPPED:	Not handicapped accessible
DIETARY NEEDS:	Will accommodate guests' special dietary needs

Chile Egg Puff

Makes 6 Servings

Easy and healthful, and a special way to serve eggs. Leftovers are great for dinner. Serve the puff with the black bean sauce for a filling dish.

5   eggs
½   teaspoon baking powder
¼   cup flour
¼   teaspoon salt
1   cup small curd cottage cheese
2   cups grated Monterey jack cheese
½   stick (¼ cup) butter, melted and cooled
½   (4-ounce) can diced green chilies, drained, or more to taste
Black bean sauce (recipe follows)

Preheat oven to 350°F. In a large bowl, beat eggs until light and lemon colored. Thoroughly mix in the rest of the ingredients, except chilies. Stir in chilies. Pour egg mixture into a buttered quiche dish or an 8x8-inch glass baking dish. Bake, uncovered, for about 35 minutes. Top should be browned and the center firm. Serve with black bean sauce.

Black bean sauce:
¼   yellow onion, chopped
2   cloves garlic, minced
1   tablespoon olive oil
1   (14-ounce) can stewed tomatoes
1   (14-ounce) can black beans
1   teaspoon cumin
½   teaspoon chili powder
¼   teaspoon cayenne pepper
3   tablespoons chopped fresh cilantro

Brown onion and garlic in oil. Add tomatoes and cook over medium heat until volume is reduced by half. Add black beans, cumin, chili powder and cayenne. Cover and cook for 15-20 minutes. You may need to add a little water to achieve desired consistency. Stir in cilantro just before serving.

Arbutus Lodge

❧Arbutus Lodge❧

Located on the "serene" side of the San Juan Islands, guests of the Arbutus Lodge enjoy peace and tranquillity as they stroll through sunny meadows and stately madronas. This delightful island retreat features two beautiful guest rooms.

Gourmet breakfasts highlight weekday mornings, while Sunday mornings feature delectable international-style specialties.

INNKEEPERS:	Susan Argento-Millington & Richard Millington
ADDRESS:	5767 West Side Road
	Friday Harbor, WA 98250
TELEPHONE:	(360) 378-8840; (888) 434-8840
E-MAIL:	arbutus@rockisland.com
WEBSITE:	www.arbutuslodge.com
ROOMS:	2 Rooms; Both with private baths
CHILDREN:	Children age 12 and older are welcome
ANIMALS:	Not allowed; Resident pets
HANDICAPPED:	Not handicapped accessible
DIETARY NEEDS:	Will accommodate guests' special dietary needs

Vegetable Frittata

Makes 8 Servings

A very versatile dish!

½   cup uncooked rice (or use ¾ cup leftover cooked rice)
¾   teaspoon salt, divided
3   leeks, split, rinsed and sliced crosswise
1   (10-ounce) package frozen chopped spinach, thawed and squeezed dry
2   zucchini, halved lengthwise, sliced crosswise
2   large carrots, grated
3   large cloves garlic, minced
2   ounces feta cheese, crumbled
3   tablespoons grated Parmesan cheese, divided
3   large eggs
9   egg whites
2   tablespoons chopped fresh mint
¾   teaspoon black pepper
2   plum tomatoes, sliced

In a small saucepan, cook rice as directed on package, using ½ teaspoon salt and no butter. Preheat broiler.

Coat a large nonstick skillet with nonstick cooking spray. Over medium heat, cook leeks, covered, for 5 minutes. Add spinach, zucchini, carrots and garlic; cook for 3 minutes. Remove vegetables to a bowl. Stir in cooked rice, feta cheese, 2 tablespoons of Parmesan cheese and ¼ teaspoon salt. Set aside.

In a medium bowl, whisk or beat eggs, egg whites, mint and pepper. Coat a large ovenproof skillet with nonstick cooking spray. Over medium-high heat, add vegetable mixture, spreading evenly; pour in egg mixture. Cook 2 minutes, lifting at edges. Cover and cook 3 minutes more. Place skillet 3 to 4 inches under broiler, for 5 minutes, or until brown. Remove from oven, arrange tomato slices on top and sprinkle with remaining Parmesan cheese. Return to oven and broil until cheese is melted. Serve.

Old Consulate Inn
(F.W. Hastings House)

Sitting high on a bluff with commanding views of Port Townsend Bay, Mount Rainier and the Olympic Mountains, the Old Consulate Inn is Port Townsend's founding family mansion. Originally built in 1889 by Senator F.W. Hastings, this grand mansion has become one of the most photographed and artistically depicted Victorians in the Pacific Northwest.

The Old Consulate Inn is a designated National Historic Landmark.

INNKEEPERS:	Michael DeLong
ADDRESS:	313 Walker at Washington
	Port Townsend, WA 98368
TELEPHONE:	(360) 385-6753; (800) 300-6753
E-MAIL:	anyone@oldconsulateinn.com
WEBSITE:	www.oldconsulateinn.com
ROOMS:	8 Rooms; All with private baths
CHILDREN:	Children age 12 and older are welcome
ANIMALS:	Not allowed
HANDICAPPED:	Not handicapped accessible
DIETARY NEEDS:	Will accommodate guests' special dietary needs

Frittata Italiano

Makes 2 (10-inch) Frittatas (Makes 8 Servings Each)

We begin this breakfast with wedges of cantaloupe wrapped in prosciutto and topped with crumbles of gorgonzola cheese, and offer side dishes of baked Italian link sausage, thin-sliced provolone cheese and Roma Romano Tomatoes (see recipe on page 195)." ~ Old Consulate Inn

¾   pound Italian sausage
⅓   cup diced (¼-inch) onion
⅓   cup diced (¼-inch) green bell pepper
⅓   cup diced (¼-inch) sun-dried tomatoes
2   cloves roasted garlic, mashed (optional, but wonderful – see page 221)
2   cups cubed potatoes (small cubes)
10   eggs, beaten
¾   cup sour cream
2   cups (or a little more) grated Monterey Jack cheese
1   cup grated (not finely) Parmigiano-Reggiano cheese, divided
3   tablespoons diced pepperoncini (optional)
1   teaspoon basil
1   teaspoon oregano
Salt and pepper, to taste
2   tablespoons butter
¼   cup sliced black olives (garnish)
2   sprigs fresh basil (garnish)

In a medium skillet, lightly brown sausage; drain and set aside. In same pan, cook onion and green pepper until translucent. Add sun-dried tomatoes and garlic during last minute or two; set aside. Cook potatoes just until done, but not soft; set aside. In a large bowl, combine eggs, sour cream, Monterey Jack cheese and ¾ cup of Parmesan cheese. Stir in sausage, onion mixture, potatoes and pepperoncini. Season with basil, oregano, salt and pepper.

Preheat oven to 350°F. Melt butter in 2 (10-inch) ovenproof skillets. Divide frittata mixture between pans; cook over medium heat for about 10 minutes, or until edges are starting to set and center is still undone. Gently shake pans occasionally to prevent sticking. Put pans in oven for 5-10 minutes, until center of frittata is set. Slide onto serving platter. Cut each frittata into 8 wedges. Garnish with remaining ¼ cup Parmesan cheese, olives and basil.

The Highland Inn

Orca whales are easily seen and heard from the Highland Inn's expansive decks. Bald eagles, owls and myriad other birds find nests along the inn's coastline. Whale Watch Park and the Lime Kiln Lighthouse are just a mile up the coast with many hiking trails and picnic spots along the way.

"It's all about luxury at the Highland Inn. Think of this B&B on the nature-loving west coast as the Four Season of San Juan Island" ~ *Travel Holiday Magazine*

INNKEEPERS:	Helen King
ADDRESS:	PO Box 135
	Friday Harbor, WA 98250
TELEPHONE:	(360) 378-9450; (888) 400-9850
E-MAIL:	helen@highlandinn.com
WEBSITE:	www.highlandinn.com
ROOMS:	2 Suites; Both with private baths
CHILDREN:	Not allowed
ANIMALS:	Not allowed
HANDICAPPED:	Not handicapped accessible
DIETARY NEEDS:	Will accommodate guests' special dietary needs

Artichoke Frittata

Makes 12 Servings

16   ounces frozen artichoke hearts, thawed (or canned, drained)
1   onion, chopped
1   tablespoon butter
1¼   cups half & half
6   eggs
1   tablespoon Worcestershire sauce
2   teaspoons Coleman's mustard (dry, not prepared)
1   teaspoon seasoning salt
2   English muffins, broken up into pieces
¼   cup Italian bread crumbs
Paprika, optional
Chopped parsley, optional
½   pound Monterey Jack cheese, grated
¼   cup grated Parmesan cheese

Chop artichoke hearts in blender or Cuisinart. Butter an 8-inch or 9-inch square pan (or use individual ramekins). Spread artichokes into bottom of pan. Cook onions in a little butter until soft, then spread over artichokes.

Preheat oven to 350°F. Blend half & half with eggs, Worcestershire, mustard and seasoning salt. Pour half of egg mixture over artichokes. In blender, blend English muffins into other half of egg mixture until smooth. Pour the muffin/egg mixture over artichokes. Sprinkle bread crumbs over the mixture. Sprinkle with paprika and chopped parsley, if desired.

Bake for 20 minutes. Remove from oven and sprinkle with Monterey Jack and Parmesan cheeses. Bake for 25-40 minutes more, until center is set. Cool slightly and cut into squares.

Kangaroo House

P ut your feet up in the spacious living room of the Kangaroo House with its grand, fieldstone fireplace and turn-of-the-century furnishings. Spend a quiet afternoon curled up with a book. Enjoy the casual homemade breakfast in the bright airy breakfast room or on the sunny deck.

"The Kangaroo House is my favorite hotel in the world! The breakfast was fantastic! I hope to come here more often." ~ Natalie, Kangaroo House guest, age 9

INNKEEPERS:	Peter & Helen Allen
ADDRESS:	1459 North Beach Road, PO Box 334
	Eastsound, WA 98245
TELEPHONE:	(360) 376-2175; (888) 371-2175
E-MAIL:	innkeeper@kangaroohouse.com
WEBSITE:	www.kangaroohouse.com
ROOMS:	4 Rooms; 1 Suite; Private and shared baths
CHILDREN:	Welcome
ANIMALS:	Not allowed
HANDICAPPED:	Not handicapped accessible
DIETARY NEEDS:	Will accommodate guests' special dietary needs

Mediterranean Frittata

Makes 6 Servings

1	teaspoon olive oil
1	small onion, diced
2	cloves garlic, minced
6	red potatoes, parboiled (quartered as necessary)
4	ounces pancetta (or cooked ham), diced
1	cup artichoke hearts, quartered
10	large eggs, beaten
4	dashes Tabasco pepper sauce
1	tablespoon chiffonade (thinly sliced strips) fresh basil

Salt and pepper, to taste

1	cup grated provolone cheese

Sour cream, for garnish

Herbs, such as chives, Italian parsley, etc., for garnish

6	slices tomato, for garnish

Preheat oven to 350°F. Heat olive oil in a large, nonstick, ovenproof skillet. Cook onion and garlic until softened. Add potatoes, pancetta and artichoke hearts; cook for a couple of minutes. Whisk together eggs, Tabasco, basil, salt and pepper. Pour over mixture in pan and cook, lifting cooked edges with a spatula and allowing uncooked portion of eggs to run underneath.

Put pan in oven and bake for 8 to 10 minutes, or until egg on top is cooked. Invert onto serving plate, cut in wedges and sprinkle with grated cheese. Garnish the frittata with sour cream, herbs and tomato slices. Serve immediately.

Chambered Nautilus

The Chambered Nautilus is a classic Seattle-style bed and breakfast inn that combines the warmth of a country inn with excellent access to the city's theaters, restaurants and shopping areas. Architecturally, this Georgian Colonial reflects the English heritage of its original owners.

Catering services can be made available for events held at the inn.

INNKEEPERS:	Joyce Schulte & Steven Poole
ADDRESS:	5005 22nd Avenue NE
	Seattle, WA 98105
TELEPHONE:	(206) 522-2536; (800) 545-8459
E-MAIL:	stay@chamberednautilus.com
WEBSITE:	www.chamberednautilus.com
ROOMS:	10 Rooms; 4 Suites; All with private baths
CHILDREN:	Call ahead
ANIMALS:	Not allowed
HANDICAPPED:	Not handicapped accessible
DIETARY NEEDS:	Will accommodate guests' special dietary needs

Northwest Salmon Breakfast Pie

Makes 6 Servings

Don't let the name fool you. This quiche-like treat can be served for any meal! Paired with a fresh tossed salad or a colorful fruit plate, it will make a delightful lunch or casual dinner.

1	unbaked ready-made pie crust
1	cup chopped onion
1	clove garlic, minced
3	tablespoons butter
5	eggs, beaten
2¼	cups sour cream
¼	cup flour
12	ounces cooked salmon, skin and bones removed, flaked
1½	grated Swiss cheese, divided
1	teaspoon dried dill weed

Paprika (optional)

Preheat oven to 400°F. Bake pie crust in a regular 10-inch pie pan (or a 9-inch deep-dish pie pan) for 8 minutes; remove from oven.

Lower oven temperature to 375°F. In a small pan, cook onion and garlic in butter until tender. In a large bowl, combine eggs, sour cream and flour. Stir in onion mixture and flaked salmon. Stir in 1 cup of cheese and dill. Pour filling into partially-baked crust. Sprinkle with remaining ½ cup cheese. Sprinkle with a little paprika for color, if desired.

Bake for 45-50 minutes (if using a deep-dish pie pan, bake for 55-60 minutes). Cover with foil for the last 15 minutes of baking time. Bake until a knife inserted in center comes out clean. Let stand 15 minutes before serving.

Turtleback Farm Inn

Located on beautiful Orcas Island, the Turtleback Farm Inn is a haven for discriminating travelers who enjoy comfortable accommodations, breathtaking scenery, varied outdoor activities, unique shopping and fine food. This historic inn overlooks 80 acres of forest and farmland in the shadow of Turtleback Mountain.

The scenery is serene, complete with a fringe of fir trees that frame the plush fields that produce bales of hay for the resident sheep.

INNKEEPERS:	William & Susan C. Fletcher
ADDRESS:	1981 Crow Valley Road
	Eastsound (Orcas Island), WA 98245
TELEPHONE:	(360) 376-4914; (800) 376-4914 (reservations)
E-MAIL:	info@turtlebackinn.com
WEBSITE:	www.turtlebackinn.com
ROOMS:	11 Rooms; All with private baths
CHILDREN:	Children age 8 and older are welcome
ANIMALS:	Not allowed; Resident dog, sheep, cows, chickens
HANDICAPPED:	Is handicapped accessible
DIETARY NEEDS:	Will accommodate guests' special dietary needs

Savory Torte

Makes 8 Servings

For years, we have offered our Smoked Salmon Torte for breakfast. It blends a smoked salmon filling with buckwheat crêpes stacked 6 high. This Savory Torte offers a different flavor combination and can be served for breakfast or luncheon.

Egg Crêpes:
1   cup milk
1   cup unbleached white flour
4   eggs
2   tablespoons butter, melted, plus ½ teaspoon butter, chilled
Pinch salt

Blend milk, flour, eggs, melted butter and salt in a blender; let sit for about 10 minutes (the batter should resemble heavy cream). Heat the ½ teaspoon butter in a 10-inch nonstick skillet over medium high heat. While tilting the pan, add just enough batter to thinly cover the bottom. Cook until bubbles pop, about 1 minute. Turn the crêpe and brown the other side. This recipe should yield 6 large crêpes.

Torte Filling:
1   bunch spinach, cleaned, stemmed and chopped (or 1 (10-ounce) package frozen chopped spinach, thawed)
½   pound mushrooms, chopped
2   tablespoons butter
8   ounces cream cheese, room temperature, cut into 8 pieces
¼   teaspoon nutmeg
Salt and pepper

Preheat oven to 350°F. Cook spinach and mushrooms in butter until tender and most of the moisture has evaporated. Add cream cheese and nutmeg; mix well. Season with salt and pepper. Cook until cream cheese is combined into the mixture. Keep warm.

Place a large rectangle of foil on counter. Place a cooked crêpe in middle of foil. Spread ⅓ heaping cup of filling over crêpe and top with second crêpe. Repeat until you have 5 crêpes covered with spinach/mushroom mixture. Top with final crêpe and seal in foil. Bake for about 15 minutes, until torte is heated through. Cut into 8 wedges. Serve with a dollop of sour cream and snipped chives or a few snipped green onion tops.

Glenna's Guthrie Cottage

Glenna's Guthrie Cottage is a rare bed and breakfast inn that offers cooking classes for its guests. Innkeeper Glenna O'Neil is a member of the American Culinary Federation. Her classes range from "Cooking by the Seat of Your Pants" for beginning cooks to low fat/low cholesterol meals, stir fry, vegetarian and Italian.

A gift area showcases antiques, quilts, dolls, tapestries, thimbles, teapots, coffees and other items.

INNKEEPERS:	Jack & Glenna O'Neil
ADDRESS:	10083 Old Olympic Highway
	Sequim, WA 98382
TELEPHONE:	(360) 681-4349
E-MAIL:	glennas.olypen.com
WEBSITE:	www.olypen.com/glennas
ROOMS:	4 Rooms; 2 Suites; Private and shared baths
CHILDREN:	Welcome
ANIMALS:	Not allowed
HANDICAPPED:	Is handicapped accessible; 1 Room
DIETARY NEEDS:	Will accommodate guests' special dietary needs

Impossible Crab Pie

Makes 6 Servings

½ pound fresh or 1 (6-ounce) can crabmeat, drained
½ cup grated cheddar cheese
1 (3-ounce) package cream cheese, room temperature
¼ cup sliced green onion
1 (2-ounce) jar diced pimientos
1 cup milk
½ cup baking mix (such as Bisquick)
2 eggs
Salt, to taste
Dash of nutmeg

Preheat oven to 350°F. In a large bowl, mix together crab, cheddar cheese, cream cheese, green onion and pimientos.

In a blender, combine milk, baking mix, eggs, salt and nutmeg. Blend on high speed for 15 seconds, then combine with crab mixture. Spoon mixture into a greased casserole dish. Place casserole dish in a pan with hot water and bake for 40 minutes.

Caswell's on the Bay

Caswell's on the Bay Bed and Breakfast is a grand, two-story turreted Victorian encircled by a covered verandah that showcases colorful flower pots and hanging baskets. The rooms are spacious, providing a wondrous setting to display quality antiques, floral and country garden watercolors and Tiffany-style stained glass lamps.

The beautifully presented breakfasts sometimes include oysters from the Willapa Bay area.

INNKEEPERS:	Bob & Marilyn Caswell
ADDRESS:	25204 Sandridge Road
	Ocean Park, WA 98640
TELEPHONE:	(360) 665-6535; (888) 553-2319
E-MAIL:	bcaswell@willapabay.org
WEBSITE:	www.caswellsinn.com
ROOMS:	5 Rooms; All with private baths
CHILDREN:	Children age 12 and older are welcome
ANIMALS:	Not allowed
HANDICAPPED:	Not handicapped accessible
DIETARY NEEDS:	Will accommodate guests' special dietary needs

Shredded Potato Quiche

Makes 8 Servings

"Real men" do eat quiche ... and here's a very hearty and flavorful one! Start this recipe the night before you plan to serve it. For vegetarian guests, leave out the bacon, or try substituting chopped canned artichoke hearts for the bacon.

3-4	cups (12-16 ounces) frozen seasoned shredded potatoes (tiny Tater Tots or Crispy Crowns work great)
¼	cup grated Parmesan cheese
½	cup sliced green onions
½	cup grated Swiss cheese
½	cup grated Monterey Jack cheese
1	cup grated cheddar cheese
½	pound bacon (8-10 slices), cooked and crumbled
1	(3-ounce) can sliced mushrooms, drained
¼	cup (or more) sliced zucchini
¼	cup (or more) diced yellow or red bell pepper
5	eggs
2	cups half & half
¾	teaspoon salt
¼	teaspoon sugar
⅛	teaspoon cayenne pepper

Preheat broiler. Coat a 10-inch deep dish pie pan with nonstick cooking spray. Place potatoes in pie pan and broil, stirring occasionally, until all sides of potatoes are browned. Mash potatoes with fork to cover bottom of pan. Over potatoes, layer Parmesan cheese, green onions, Swiss cheese, Monterey Jack cheese, cheddar cheese, bacon, mushrooms, zucchini and bell pepper. Cover and refrigerate overnight.

Next morning: Preheat oven to 375°F. In a large bowl, beat together eggs, half & half, salt, sugar and cayenne pepper. Pour egg mixture slowly over top of refrigerated quiche ingredients. Bake for 50-60 minutes, or until golden brown and a knife inserted in center comes out clean. Remove from oven and let stand for 20 minutes before serving.

Stratford Manor

Enjoy park-like grounds, of this 30 acre manor with a large pond where migrating birds congregate in the spring. Guests can paddle boat in the summer, pick apples in the orchard in the fall and enjoy the colorful perennial flower beds from spring through fall.

Winter offers the comfort of the library with a good book or a romantic movie.

INNKEEPERS:	Leslie & Jim Lohse
ADDRESS:	4566 Anderson Way
	Bellingham, WA 98226
TELEPHONE:	(360) 715-8441; (800) 240-6779
E-MAIL:	llohse@aol.com
WEBSITE:	www.stratfordmanor.com
ROOMS:	3 Rooms; All with private baths
CHILDREN:	Not allowed
ANIMALS:	Not allowed
HANDICAPPED:	Not handicapped accessible
DIETARY NEEDS:	Will accommodate guests' special dietary needs

Salmon Quiche

Makes 8 Servings

This recipe is a perfect way to use up left-over salmon.

8   eggs
1½   cups milk
½   cup flour
1½   teaspoons baking powder
2   cups flaked cooked salmon fillet (about 1 pound salmon fillet)
      (or substitute canned salmon)
1½   cups grated cheddar cheese
2   green onions, thickly sliced
1   stick (½ cup) butter, melted
Salt and pepper, to taste

Preheat oven to 350°F. Beat eggs and milk together. Add flour and baking
powder; mix well. Stir in salmon, cheese, green onions, butter, salt and
pepper. Pour into a 10-inch quiche pan which has been sprayed with
nonstick cooking spray. Bake for 45 to 50 minutes. Let stand for 10
minutes before serving.

Salisbury House

S alisbury House Bed and Breakfast Inn offers gracious accommodations for the discerning traveler. Situated on a tree-lined residential street, this urban bed and breakfast is only minutes from downtown Seattle, the University of Washington and Seattle University.

The public rooms are large and bright. A well-stocked library has a game table for an evening of chess or a morning of writing postcards by the fire.

INNKEEPERS:	Cathryn & Mary Wiese
ADDRESS:	750 16th Avenue East
	Seattle, WA 98112
TELEPHONE:	(206) 328-8682
E-MAIL:	sleep@salisburyhouse.com
WEBSITE:	www.salisburyhouse.com
ROOMS:	5 Rooms; All with private baths
CHILDREN:	Children age 12 and older are welcome
ANIMALS:	Not allowed
HANDICAPPED:	Not handicapped accessible
DIETARY NEEDS:	Will accommodate guests' special dietary needs

Winter Quiche with Leeks and Brie

Makes 4 Servings

Crust:

½   cup flour
3   tablespoons unsalted butter, chilled
1   tablespoon vegetable shortening, chilled
¼   cup ice water, or less

Filling:

2   cups thinly sliced leeks (about 2 large leeks), use only white and light green parts, rinsed well in sieve and shaken dry
1   small clove garlic, minced
2   tablespoons olive oil
3   eggs
½   cup milk or half & half
¼   teaspoon dried thyme (or ½ teaspoon chopped fresh)
¼   teaspoon dried sage (or ½ teaspoon chopped fresh)
Salt and pepper, to taste
½   cup cubed Brie cheese (about 3 ounces)

For the crust: Preheat oven to 425°F. In a medium bowl, mix flour, butter and shortening with a pastry blender or fork. Slowly add ice water, a little at a time, until mixture begins to hold together. Form ball with hands, handling as little as possible, adding only enough water to keep mixture together. Roll out dough on a lightly floured surface. Place in an 8-inch pie pan or a 9-inch tart pan. Bake for about 5 to 10 minutes, until crust browns slightly.

For the filling: While crust is baking, cook leeks and garlic in olive oil until tender; remove from heat. In a small bowl, mix eggs, milk, thyme, sage, salt and pepper. Into partially cooked crust, spread cooked leeks and garlic; sprinkle evenly with chunks of brie. Pour egg mixture over top.

Bake for 15 minutes at 425°F. Lower heat to 350°F and bake for about 10 minutes more, or until quiche is set and top is slightly browned. Let cool for about 5 minutes before serving.

Autumn Pond

Autumn Pond rests on three quiet country acres, surrounded by panoramic views of the majestic Cascades. The location is perfect for a brisk walk to downtown or a quiet evening stroll to the Ski Hill area where wild flowers will delight your senses. There is also a large pond with fishing, ducks and bird watching.

The town of Leavenworth has a number of Bavarian Festivals, including Autumn Leaf, Salmon Festival, Bon Appétit Gala and Christkindlmarkt.

INNKEEPERS:	John & Jennifer Lorenz
ADDRESS:	10388 Titus Road
	Leavenworth, WA 98826
TELEPHONE:	(509) 548-4482; (800) 222-9661
E-MAIL:	info@autumnpond.com
WEBSITE:	www.autumnpond.com
ROOMS:	5 Rooms; All with private baths
CHILDREN:	Children age 10 and older are welcome
ANIMALS:	Not allowed; Resident dogs
HANDICAPPED:	Not handicapped accessible
DIETARY NEEDS:	Will accommodate guests' special dietary needs

Cinnamon Bread Soufflé with Buttered Maple Syrup

Makes 6 Servings

If you are on a diet, take a day off – this decadent treat is well worth it! It is also very easy to make – put it together the day before and pop it in the oven an hour before serving. Use your favorite cinnamon bread, with or without raisins. This recipe can be easily doubled and baked in a 9x13-inch baking dish.

1	loaf cinnamon bread, cut into 1-inch cubes
5	large eggs
1½	cups half & half
1½	cups maple syrup, divided
6	ounces cream cheese, room temperature
3	tablespoons plus 1 stick (½ cup) butter, room temperature

Cinnamon for dusting
Powdered sugar for dusting

Butter an 8x8-inch baking dish (or a 1 quart casserole dish). Line the bottom with bread cubes up to 2 layers thick (you may have leftover bread).

Beat eggs, half & half and ⅓ cup of maple syrup until well blended, then pour over bread cubes. Beat cream cheese, 3 tablespoons butter and 3 tablespoons maple syrup together until fluffy. Spread over top of bread/egg mixture. Dust with cinnamon and cover with plastic wrap. Refrigerate overnight.

In the morning, preheat oven to 350°F. Remove soufflé from refrigerator and uncover. Bake for 55 to 60 minutes, until center of soufflé is set.

Heat remaining maple syrup (about 1 cup) and the 1 stick of butter until butter is melted. Dust finished soufflé with powdered sugar and cut into squares. Serve hot, accompanied by the hot buttered maple syrup.

Boreas Inn

Innkeepers Susie Goldsmith and Bill Verner's warm hospitality will make your stay at the Boreas Bed and Breakfast Inn memorable, and the culinary feasts they prepare for you in the morning will delight your palate. Ensuring privacy, only an expanse of sand and grasses separate the inn from the ocean. You truly will feel like this is your private oceanfront getaway.

Boreas' morning feasts are a culinary treat. Enjoy smoked salmon caught by local fishermen and oysters from local Willapa and Shoalwater Bays.

INNKEEPERS:	Susie Goldsmith & Bill Verner
ADDRESS:	607 North Ocean Beach Boulevard
	Long Beach, WA 98631
TELEPHONE:	(888) 642-8069
E-MAIL:	boreas@boreasinn.com
WEBSITE:	www.boreasinn.com
ROOMS:	5 Suites; All with private baths
CHILDREN:	Call ahead
ANIMALS:	Not allowed
HANDICAPPED:	Not handicapped accessible
DIETARY NEEDS:	Will accommodate guests' special dietary needs

Boreas Apple Cinnamon Breakfast Bread Pudding

Serves 8 to 12

This breakfast treat can be made the night before and baked in the morning.

15 slices apple cinnamon (or cinnamon raisin) bread
5   eggs
3   cups half & half
1   cup sugar
1   tablespoon grated orange zest
2   teaspoons vanilla (Grand Marnier or rum may be substituted)
Plain or vanilla yogurt (optional)

Grease an 9x13-inch baking dish. Preheat oven to 350°F. Tear bread into bite-size pieces and place in greased dish. In a medium mixing bowl, combine eggs, half & half, sugar, orange zest and vanilla; pour over bread.

Bake, uncovered, for about 45 minutes, or until a knife inserted in center comes out clean. Let stand 15 minutes before cutting and serving. Serve with yogurt if desired.

Angelica's

Built in 1907 by renowned Spokane architect Kirtland Cutter, Angelica's Bed and Breakfast is an exquisitely appointed turn-of-the-twentieth-century home. Gleaming woodwork, antique furnishings, period lighting and diamond-paned, leaded glass windows combine to create a warm and inviting atmosphere.

This elegant brick mansion is listed on the local and National Register of Historic Places.

INNKEEPERS:	**Lynette & Ted Gustafson**
ADDRESS:	**1321 West 9th Avenue**
	Spokane, WA 99204
TELEPHONE:	**(509) 624-5598**
E-MAIL:	**info@angelicasbb.com**
WEBSITE:	**www.angelicasbb.com**
ROOMS:	2 Rooms; 2 Suites; All with private baths
CHILDREN:	Children age 12 and older are welcome
ANIMALS:	Not allowed; Resident cat
HANDICAPPED:	Not handicapped accessible
DIETARY NEEDS:	Will accommodate guests' special dietary needs

Raspberry Apple-Stuffed Croissant

Serves 6 to 8

"On a trip to Arizona, we were served a dish similar to this, and I thought it would be a great addition to our repertoire. I've adapted it and now serve it here – our guests love it! Serve the croissant on a pool of crème Anglaise for an elegant touch." ~ Lynette Gustafson, Angelica's.

6-8   freshly baked croissants
1-2   Granny Smith apples, thinly sliced
1   teaspoon cinnamon
½   teaspoon nutmeg
2   tablespoons sugar
2   eggs
½   cup half & half
1   teaspoon vanilla
1-2   slices Canadian bacon per croissant
6-8   slices Muenster cheese (1 slice per croissant)
Raspberry Ambrosia (recipe follows)

Preheat oven to 350°F. Slice croissants lengthwise and tear out the dough portion. Toss apple slices with cinnamon, nutmeg and sugar; set aside.

Whisk together eggs, half & half and vanilla in a shallow dish. On croissant bottoms, place slices of Canadian bacon, apple slices and a slice of cheese. Dip croissant tops in egg mixture and place atop cheese. Place croissant on a lightly greased cookie sheet and bake for 30 minutes.

Place a small pool of crème Anglaise on each serving plate. Place croissants on top of crème anglaise. Drizzle Raspberry Ambrosia over each croissant.

Raspberry Ambrosia:
2   cups fresh or frozen raspberries
1   tablespoon cornstarch
1   teaspoon lemon juice
½   cup sugar
1   teaspoon cinnamon

In a small saucepan over medium heat, combine all ingredients. Cook until mixture thickens. Add more sugar, if desired. A touch of brandy is a nice addition, if desired.

Fruit Specialties

Fruit Specialties

Bosch Gärten

Built in 1992 specifically as a bed and breakfast, Bosch Gärten provides a quiet getaway with the magnificent Cascade Mountains towering in the background. Guests enjoy the living room with its 30-foot ceiling, distinctive fireplace and 18-foot potted Norfolk pine.

The fresh, multi-course breakfast features Leavenworth's fabulous tree fruits, pastries, juice, tea and freshly ground Starbucks coffee.

INNKEEPERS:	Georgeanne & Denny Nichols
ADDRESS:	9846 Dye Road
	Leavenworth, WA 98826
TELEPHONE:	(509) 548-6900; (800) 535-0069
E-MAIL:	innkeeper@boschgarten.com
WEBSITE:	www.boschgarten.com.com
ROOMS:	3 Rooms; All with private baths
CHILDREN:	Call ahead
ANIMALS:	Not allowed
HANDICAPPED:	Not handicapped accessible
DIETARY NEEDS:	Will accommodate guests' special dietary needs

Fresh Fruit with Amaretto Cream

Makes 4 Servings

"We use blueberries, green grapes, apples, peaches, bananas, strawberries and pears – any combination of fresh fruit will work. The sauce keeps for two weeks, so we make double batches." ~ Bosch Gärten Bed & Breakfast

1½ tablespoons amaretto liqueur
2   tablespoons dark brown sugar
½   cup sour cream
2   cups cut-up fresh fruit

In a small bowl, stir together liqueur and brown sugar. Add sour cream and mix thoroughly. Chill in refrigerator for 2 hours before serving. Place ½ cup of fruit into each serving dish (use pretty sherbet glasses). Drizzle with sauce just before serving.

Boreas Inn

Situated near the rugged Pacific Ocean, the Boreas Bed and Breakfast Inn is a romantic bed and breakfast that features spectacular ocean views and sumptuous gourmet breakfasts. Located in a quiet neighborhood, this artistically remodeled, 1920s beach home boasts a therapeutic spa enclosed in a totally private, cedar and glass gazebo.

"You have the most awesome place in Long Beach." ~ Guest, Boreas Bed and Breakfast Inn

INNKEEPERS:	Susie Goldsmith & Bill Verner
ADDRESS:	607 North Ocean Beach Boulevard
	Long Beach, WA 98631
TELEPHONE:	(888) 642-8069
E-MAIL:	boreas@boreasinn.com
WEBSITE:	www.boreasinn.com
ROOMS:	5 Suites; All with private baths
CHILDREN:	Call ahead
ANIMALS:	Not allowed
HANDICAPPED:	Not handicapped accessible
DIETARY NEEDS:	Will accommodate guests' special dietary needs

Boreas Stuffed Cranberry Butter Rum Pears

Makes 4 Servings

This recipe utilizes Washington's wonderful pears and the Long Beach Peninsula's delicious cranberries. Choose pears that are fragrant and free of blemishes or soft spots. This is one of Boreas' most requested recipes. The dish may be prepared the night before and covered tightly with plastic wrap to allow the rum to permeate the pears. However, do not bake it until just before serving.

4	ripe, but not over-ripe, Washington Bartlett or Bosc pears, peeled and cored
¼	cup brown sugar
¼	teaspoon cinnamon
⅛	teaspoon freshly grated nutmeg
½	cup dried cranberries
½	cup pecans
⅓	cup dark rum
4	teaspoons butter

Caramel apple dipping sauce (available at most groceries)
Springs of fresh mint, to garnish

Preheat oven to 350°F. Mix together brown sugar, cinnamon, nutmeg, cranberries and pecans. Stuff ¼ of brown sugar mixture into each pear, packing lightly. Place pears in a baking dish. Pour rum over top of pears. Put about ½-inch of water in dish. Top each pear with 1 teaspoon butter.

Put pears in oven. While baking, baste pears occasionally and rotate them at least once to assure even baking on all sides. When pears are tender, about 20-25 minutes, remove from oven and place on serving dishes.

While pears are still very hot, top each pear with ½-1 teaspoon caramel apple dipping sauce and then pour a little sauce from the pan over each pear. Serve warm, garnished with a sprig of fresh mint.

A Touch of Europe

Built in 1889 by one of Yakima's prominent pioneers, A Touch of Europe Bed and Breakfast Inn eventually became the home of Mrs. Ina Phillips Williams, Yakima County's first woman legislator in the Washington State House of Representatives. Every room is rich in history. Theodore Roosevelt once met with Mrs. Williams in the library.

This Queen Anne Victorian house is on the National Register of Historic Places.

INNKEEPERS:	Erika G. & James A. Cenci
ADDRESS:	220 North 16th Avenue
	Yakima, WA 98902
TELEPHONE:	(509) 454-9775; (888) 438-7073
E-MAIL:	atoeurope@msn.com
WEBSITE:	www.winesnw.com/toucheuropeb&b.htm
ROOMS:	3 Rooms; All with private baths
CHILDREN:	Not allowed
ANIMALS:	Not allowed
HANDICAPPED:	Not handicapped accessible
DIETARY NEEDS:	Will accommodate guests' special dietary needs

Signature Pears in Amaretto with Chocolate Sauce

Makes 4 Servings

4   large pears
Cold water
Juice of 1 lemon
4   tablespoons sugar
1   cup water
4   tablespoons amaretto liqueur
1   cup chocolate sauce, warm (recipe follows)
Whipped cream, for garnish
Peppermint leaves, for garnish
½   cup sliced almonds, for garnish

Carefully peel pears, leaving stems intact. Place peeled whole pears in a large bowl. Fill with cold water, add lemon juice and set aside. In a large saucepan, bring sugar and 1 cup water to a boil over medium-high heat. Drain pears and place them on their sides in the sugar water. Add liqueur, lower heat and simmer, covered, for 20 minutes. Carefully transfer pears to a serving dish and ladle sugar water/liqueur mixture over them. Let pears cool, then cover and refrigerate overnight. Drain pears before serving.

For a beautiful presentation: Place each pear in an individual glass dish, then set each dish on a big plate. Serve with warm chocolate sauce, a dollop of whipped cream and garnish with mint leaves and sliced almonds.

Chocolate sauce:
8   ounces semi-sweet chocolate, cut into bits
½   cup strong brewed coffee
1   teaspoon amaretto liqueur or cognac

In top of double boiler over hot water, melt chocolate with coffee and liqueur. Keep sauce warm over hot water until serving. If sauce becomes too thick, thin it with more coffee. Note: Recipe may be doubled.

Lietz's

Lietz's Bed and Breakfast is a cozy country inn located four and one-half miles east of Leavenworth on the Wenatchee River. Guests savor the delicious, family-style breakfast that is served each morning from seven to ten o'clock.

Due to the close proximity of the Wenatchee River, guests can experience venturesome innertube float trips, the innertubes being provided by the inn.

INNKEEPERS:	Verne & Helen Lietz
ADDRESS:	8305 Lynn Street
	Peshastin, WA 98847
TELEPHONE:	(509) 548-7504
E-MAIL:	lietzaire@linear.com
WEBSITE:	Not available
ROOMS:	3 Rooms; All with shared baths
CHILDREN:	Welcome
ANIMALS:	Not allowed
HANDICAPPED:	Is handicapped accessible
DIETARY NEEDS:	Will accommodate guests' special dietary needs

Pears Extraordinaire

Makes 2 Servings

The rich, red color of the berries contrast the green of the mint leaves for a beautiful presentation.

1   pear, peeled, halved lengthwise and cored
2   tablespoons apple juice or favorite liqueur (green-colored crème de menthe is great at Christmas)
1   tablespoon cream cheese, room temperature
1   teaspoon honey
¼   teaspoon vanilla
Fresh red raspberries or strawberries, for garnish
Fresh mint leaves, for garnish

In a small microwave-safe dish, place pear halves cut-side down. Add apple juice or liqueur. Cover with plastic wrap and microwave for 4-5 minutes to poach the pear until soft, but not mushy. Drain off any liquid. Place each pear half, cut-side up, on individual serving plates.

In a small bowl, mix together cream cheese, honey and vanilla. Spoon half of mixture into center of each pear half. Garnish with fresh berries and mint leaves.

Stratford Manor

G uests of the Stratford Manor Bed and Breakfast can schedule a relaxing and soothing massage. The licensed massage therapist is experienced in Swedish Deep Tissue and Sport Massage and customizes his sessions to specific pains or just for mental and physical relaxation.

Sessions are for one hour or a couple's special that includes two 45-minute massages.

INNKEEPERS:	Leslie & Jim Lohse
ADDRESS:	4566 Anderson Way
	Bellingham, WA 98226
TELEPHONE:	(360) 715-8441; (800) 240-6779
E-MAIL:	llohse@aol.com
WEBSITE:	www.stratfordmanor.com
ROOMS:	3 Rooms; All with private baths
CHILDREN:	Not allowed
ANIMALS:	Not allowed
HANDICAPPED:	Not handicapped accessible
DIETARY NEEDS:	Will accommodate guests' special dietary needs

Winter Fruit Compote

Makes 4 Servings

8	prunes, pitted
8	dried apricots
1	cup apple juice
1	cinnamon stick
½	teaspoon whole cloves
½	cup orange juice
3	tablespoons orange marmalade
1	banana, peeled and sliced
1	orange, peeled and cut-up
1	apple, peeled and diced

Chopped pecans, for garnish

In a medium saucepan, combine prunes, apricots, apple juice, cinnamon stick and cloves. Bring to a boil and remove from heat. Refrigerate, letting the prunes and apricots soak in the apple juice mixture overnight.

Next morning: Place 2 prunes and 2 apricots in each of 4 serving dishes. Strain the apple juice mixture. Add orange juice and orange marmalade to apple juice mixture. Add cut-up banana, orange and apple; gently stir to mix. Divide between the serving dishes and top with chopped pecans.

Redfern Farm

Redfern Farm Bed and Breakfast is a 50-year-old, steeply gabled farmhouse surrounded by 20 acres of pasture on Puget Island in the Columbia River. The island was named in 1792 after Peter Puget and is one of a handful of the hundreds of islands in the Columbia River estuary. Drainage sloughs and a perimeter dike protect the island.

Access to the island is either by bridge from Cathlamet, Washington or by ferry from Westport, Oregon.

INNKEEPERS:	Winnie Lowsma
ADDRESS:	277 Cross Dike Road
	Cathlamet, WA 98612
TELEPHONE:	(360) 849-4108
E-MAIL:	redfernfarm@msn.com
WEBSITE:	Not available
ROOMS:	2 Rooms; Both with private baths
CHILDREN:	Children age 6 and older are welcome
ANIMALS:	Not allowed
HANDICAPPED:	Not handicapped accessible
DIETARY NEEDS:	Will accommodate guests' special dietary needs

Apple Meringue Cassolette

Makes 2 Servings

A light sweetness to start the day!

1   tablespoon frozen apple juice concentrate
3   tablespoons water
1   teaspoon cornstarch
1   medium apple, peeled and diced
2   egg whites, room temperature
1-2 teaspoons sugar
Dash of cinnamon
Sprinkle of coconut

Preheat oven to 350°F. In a small saucepan, combine apple juice concentrate, water and cornstarch. Mix well using a mini whisk. Cook over medium heat, stirring constantly, until mixture is clear, bubbling and thickened. Add apples and stir to coat with sauce. Set aside.

To make meringue: In a small bowl, beat egg whites. Add sugar and beat until stiff (whites should hold their shape); set aside.

Divide apple mixture between 2 small, ungreased cassolette dishes (or ramekins or custard cups). Dust lightly with cinnamon. Using a small spatula, spread half the meringue over the top of each filled dish, sealing egg white mixture to rim of dish. Sprinkle a little coconut over meringue. Place dishes on a baking sheet and bake for 8-10 minutes, or until tops are nicely browned.

❧ Carol's Corner
For a very special first course at breakfast, place each ramekin on top of a colorful plate, complete with paper doily. Or, if you prefer, serve the Apple Meringue Cassolette on a larger plate accompanied by an egg dish and a muffin. Served later in the day with a cookie, this would make a delightful, light dessert. So versatile!

The Purple House

Guests take a trip back in time to a gentler, more gracious way of living when staying at The Purple House Bed and Breakfast. This elegantly remodeled Queen Anne mansion was built in 1882 by Dr. Pietrzycki, a Dayton pioneer physician and philanthropist.

The city of Dayton is a historic gem, boasting two districts listed on the National Historic Register and dozens of well-preserved Victorian homes.

INNKEEPERS:	D. Christine Williscroft
ADDRESS:	415 East Clay Street
	Dayton, WA 99328
TELEPHONE:	(509) 382-3159; (800) 486-2574
E-MAIL:	Not available
WEBSITE:	www.thehowtoguys.com/Washington/
	Dayton/purplehousebb.htm
ROOMS:	4 Rooms; 2 Suites; All with private baths
CHILDREN:	Children age 16 and older are welcome
ANIMALS:	Small pets welcome; Call ahead
HANDICAPPED:	Is handicapped accessible
DIETARY NEEDS:	Will accommodate guests' special dietary needs

Pretty and Tasty Fruit Tart

Makes 6 Servings

This pastry, sprinkled with powdered sugar, may be served warm for breakfast, or try it chilled, topped with whipped cream, for an afternoon treat with coffee or tea.

Dough:
1   stick (½ cup) butter, room temperature
2   tablespoons sugar
1   cup flour
1   egg yolk
3-4 fresh apricots, halved and pitted (plums or thinly sliced apples can also be used)

Filling:
2   eggs
2   tablespoons milk
2   tablespoons sugar
5   drops almond extract
Whipped cream or powdered sugar, for garnish

To make dough: Preheat oven to 375°F. In a medium bowl, mix together butter, sugar, flour and egg yolk. Set aside.

To make filling: In a small bowl, beat together eggs, milk, sugar and almond extract. Set aside.

Press dough into a lightly greased 9x4-inch fluted tart pan. Arrange apricot halves (skin-side down, dimple-side up). Pour filling mixture over fruit and dough (fill the dimples). Bake for approximately 45 minutes. Let cool for at least 15 minutes before serving. May be served warm or cold. Top with whipped cream or dust with powdered sugar.

Trumpeter Inn

Relax and allow yourself to absorb the warmth of the Trumpeter Inn Bed and Breakfast. Watch the glorious sunrises and sunsets. Listen to the sounds of nature and marvel at its sights. Delight in the soothing hot tub in the garden.

"Fabulous! What a comfortable and beautiful home. We loved all the extra pampering, the wonderful information and the great food!" ~ Guest, Trumpeter Inn

INNKEEPERS:	Mark Zipkin & Aylene Geringer
ADDRESS:	318 Trumpeter Way
	Friday Harbor, WA 98250
TELEPHONE:	(800) 826-7926
E-MAIL:	swan@rockisland.com
WEBSITE:	www.trumpeterinn.com
ROOMS:	6 Rooms; All with private baths
CHILDREN:	Children age 12 and older are welcome
ANIMALS:	Not allowed
HANDICAPPED:	Is handicapped accessible
DIETARY NEEDS:	Will accommodate guests' special dietary needs

Fresh Fruit-Walnut Torte

Makes 8 Servings

This is a beautiful dish. In testing it, we used peaches, raspberries, blueberries and kiwis, but you can use whatever is in season at the time of baking.

Crust:

1⅓	cups all-purpose flour
3	tablespoons sugar
1	stick (½ cup) butter, chilled and cut into small pieces
1	cup ground walnuts
1	large egg yolk
⅓	cup seedless raspberry jam

Combine flour and sugar in food processor. Cut in butter until mix resembles coarse crumbs. Blend in walnuts. With machine running, add egg yolk and mix just until dough comes together. Remove dough from processor and press into bottom and an inch up sides of a 9-inch springform pan. Spread flat surface of dough with jam.

Filling:

1½	cups light brown sugar
1	large egg
1¼	cups coarsely chopped walnuts
½	cup shredded coconut
¼	cup plus 1 tablespoon all-purpose flour
½ teaspoon baking powder	
Seasonal fresh fruit	
½	cup currant jelly

Preheat oven to 350°F. Using an electric mixer, beat brown sugar and egg in a bowl until very thick, about 10 minutes. Mix in walnuts, coconut, flour and baking powder (the batter will be very thick). Spread evenly over jam in prepared crust and bake for 30 minutes. Lower oven temperature to 300°F and continue baking until filling is set and top has browned, about 25 minutes more. Arrange fresh fruit on top. Heat ½ cup current jelly and pour over fruit to glaze.

All Seasons River Inn

Each morning at the All Seasons River Inn Bed and Breakfast brings a gourmet breakfast served in the dining room. A typical breakfast includes scones, specialty juices, Mexican tamale pancakes, and German sausage, apples and potatoes.

Depending on the season, you can hike, raft, ski, shop or attend one of the many events in the town of Leavenworth. There is never a dull moment in this charming Bavarian town!

INNKEEPERS:	Kathy & Jeff Falconer
ADDRESS:	8751 Icicle Road
	Leavenworth, WA 98826
TELEPHONE:	(509) 548-1425; (800) 254-0555
E-MAIL:	info@allseasonsriverinn.com
WEBSITE:	www.allseasonsriverinn.com
ROOMS:	6 Rooms; 3 Suites; All with private baths
CHILDREN:	Children age 16 and older are welcome
ANIMALS:	Not allowed
HANDICAPPED:	Not handicapped accessible
DIETARY NEEDS:	Will accommodate guests' special dietary needs

Breakfast Squares

Makes 12 Servings

"This dish is adapted from a dessert served by a friend. I realized how much guests would enjoy this as a base for fresh fruit. I serve it topped with mango, fresh pineapple and kiwi. Crème fraîche is poured over the top and a flower or strawberry provides a colorful adornment." ~ All Seasons River Inn

1   cup flour
1   stick (½ cup) butter, room temperature
3   tablespoons powdered sugar
1   (8-ounce) package cream cheese, room temperature
½   cup sugar
2   eggs
1   tablespoon lemon juice
Crème fraîche (recipe follows)
Fresh fruit, such as berries, kiwi, peaches, pineapple, etc.

Preheat oven to 350°F. Mix together flour and butter; press into bottom of a greased, 9x9-inch glass baking dish. Bake for 10-12 minutes.

Whip together powdered sugar, cream cheese, sugar, eggs and lemon juice; pour over baked crust. Bake for 10-12 minutes. Cool and cut into 12 squares. Stack 4 squares to a layer, separated with waxed paper. Wrap in plastic wrap and store in a freezer bag in freezer. Remove 1 hour before serving. Place a square on an individual serving plate. Top with fresh fruit.

Crème fraîche:
1   cup whipping cream
1   tablespoon sour cream
¼   cup sugar
1   teaspoon vanilla

Mix whipping cream and sour cream together; leave out on counter overnight. The following morning, discard top film. Stir in sugar and vanilla. Refrigerate until using. Store leftover in an airtight container in the refrigerator. Mark the top of the container with the same "use by date" on the whipping cream and sour cream used in the recipe.

Boreas Inn

Find yourself swept away by the picture windows in the living rooms of the Boreas Bed & Breakfast Inn, with their spectacular view of the dunes and the beach. Walk just south on the Dunes Trail and you will come upon the Long Beach Boardwalk, a perfect spot for a sunset stroll.

Just outside the inn, guests can sit in the gardens or wander a lovely, private path that, within minutes, winds through the dunes to the Pacific Ocean.

INNKEEPERS:	Susie Goldsmith & Bill Verner
ADDRESS:	607 North Ocean Beach Boulevard
	Long Beach, WA 98631
TELEPHONE:	(888) 642-8069
E-MAIL:	boreas@boreasinn.com
WEBSITE:	www.boreasinn.com
ROOMS:	5 Suites; All with private baths
CHILDREN:	Call ahead
ANIMALS:	Not allowed
HANDICAPPED:	Not handicapped accessible
DIETARY NEEDS:	Will accommodate guests' special dietary needs

Grandma's Peach Kuchen

Makes 8 to 10 Servings

This was passed down from Susie Goldsmith's Grandmother. You can use fresh fruits or canned pears instead of canned peaches. You can also mix the fruits and do a combination. Italian prunes are the traditional fruit used for kuchen.

1	stick (½ cup) butter, room temperature
¼	cup sugar
1	teaspoon vanilla
2	eggs, divided
1	cup all-purpose flour
½	teaspoon baking powder
¼	teaspoon salt
1	(29-ounce) can sliced peaches, or 2 large, fresh, ripe peaches, peeled and sliced
2	tablespoons brown sugar (increase to ¼ cup if using fresh peaches)
1	teaspoon cinnamon
2	tablespoons half & half or heavy cream

Preheat oven to 350°F. Grease a 9-inch springform pan. In large bowl, beat butter and sugar until light and fluffy. Add vanilla and 1 egg; beat well. Add flour, baking powder and salt; blend well. Spread dough over bottom and 1 inch up sides of pan. Arrange peach slices in spoke fashion over dough. Sprinkle with sugar and cinnamon.

Mix 1 egg with half & half or heavy cream. Pour over peaches. Bake for 45-50 minutes, or until edges are golden brown. Cool for 10 minutes, then remove sides of pan.

Side Dishes

Side Dishes

Chinaberry Hill

Formerly called the Lucius Manning Estate, Chinaberry Hill was best known at the turn-of-the-century for its breathtaking gardens. Filled with antiques and Tacoma memorabilia, this graceful Victorian is on the National Register of Historic Places.

"Put Chinaberry Hill on wheels and we'd take it on all our vacations." ~ Guest, Chinaberry Hill

INNKEEPERS:	Cecil & Yarrow Wayman
ADDRESS:	302 Tacoma Avenue North
	North Tacoma, WA 98403
TELEPHONE:	(253) 272-1282
E-MAIL:	chinaberry@wa.net
WEBSITE:	www.chinaberryhill.com
ROOMS:	1 Room; 4 Suites; All with private baths
CHILDREN:	Children welcome in the guest cottage
ANIMALS:	Not allowed; Resident cats
HANDICAPPED:	Not handicapped accessible
DIETARY NEEDS:	Will accommodate guests' special dietary needs

Garlic Potatoes

Makes 4 to 6 Servings

"This recipe, rather embarrassingly simple, never fails to wow the crowd. Once again, as Julia Child loves to point out, people crave 'foodie food,' and that the simplest approach is often the best." ~ Cecil Wayman, Chinaberry Hill

8	small to medium potatoes (red or Yukon gold are great)
3	tablespoons butter
2	teaspoons garlic salt
1	teaspoon coarse ground pepper
3	tablespoons chopped fresh parsley

Cut potatoes into bite-sized cubes. Rinse well and pat dry. Put butter in a 12-inch skillet over medium-high to high heat. Before butter is completely melted, add potatoes. Cover and cook for 2-3 minutes. Remove lid and check to see if potatoes are browning (they should be getting pretty crispy). Check every minute or so, and stir them from the bottom every time.

Once potatoes are nicely browned, lower heat to low and keep potatoes warm until serving. Just before serving, add garlic salt, pepper and parsley. (Be sure to add garlic salt just before serving for maximum impact!)

Inn at Barnum Point

During her childhood, innkeeper Carolin Barnum Dilorenzo played on the Camano Island beach and swam and boated in Port Susan Bay. As an adult, she built a beautiful home on the edge of an orchard that overlooks Port Susan Bay and now offers her home as The Inn at Barnum Point.

On clear days, the inn offers spectacular views of Mount Rainier and the Cascades.

INNKEEPERS:	Carolin Barnum Dilorenzo
ADDRESS:	464 South Barnum Road
	Camano Island, WA 98292
TELEPHONE:	(360) 387-2256; (800) 910-2256
E-MAIL:	barnum@camano.net
WEBSITE:	www.innatbarnumpoint.com
ROOMS:	3 Rooms; All with private baths
CHILDREN:	Welcome
ANIMALS:	Not allowed
HANDICAPPED:	Not handicapped accessible
DIETARY NEEDS:	Will accommodate guests' special dietary needs

Barnum Point Potato Special

Makes 2 Servings

2   cups diced, unpeeled red potatoes, cooked
1   tablespoon vegetable or olive oil
1   small onion, diced
½   cup (total) diced mixed green, red, orange and yellow bell peppers
½   cup diced cooked ham
Salt and pepper
½   cup grated Monterey Jack cheese
½   cup grated cheddar cheese
Sour cream
Salsa

Preheat oven to 350°F. In a medium ovenproof skillet, cook potatoes in oil until browned. Add onion and peppers; cook until onions are translucent. Add ham and heat through. Season with salt and pepper. Top with cheeses and place in oven until cheese is melted.

Transfer to individual serving plates or serve directly from hot skillet at the table. (Note: If you prefer, the potatoes can also be divided between 2 individual ovenproof serving dishes before putting them in the oven.) Serve with sour cream and salsa on the side.

Four Winds Guest House

Located within walking distance of the mighty Grand Coulee Dam, the Four Winds Guest House Bed and Breakfast evokes another era in its 1930s charm and spectacular setting. Originally a dormitory for engineers working on the dam, this historic building is the last of the government built homes open to the public.

Grand Coulee Dam is home to the world's largest laser light show.

INNKEEPERS:	Dick & Fe Taylor
ADDRESS:	301 Lincoln Street
	Coulee Dam, WA 99116
TELEPHONE:	(509) 633-3146; (800) 786-3146
E-MAIL:	fourwind@cuonlinenow.com
WEBSITE:	www.fourwindsbandb.com
ROOMS:	11 Rooms; 1 Suite; Private and shared baths
CHILDREN:	Call ahead
ANIMALS:	Not allowed
HANDICAPPED:	Call ahead
DIETARY NEEDS:	Call ahead

Comeback Hash

Makes 6 Servings

A very colorful and hearty dish!

4   tablespoons butter or margarine, divided
1   (2-pound) bag frozen Southern-style hash brown potatoes
Oregano, to taste
Thyme, to taste
Basil, to taste
Garlic powder, to taste
1   medium onion, diced
½   green bell pepper, diced
½   red bell pepper, diced
5   precooked German sausages (about 4-ounces each), diced
1   (16-ounce) bag frozen corn kernels
Salsa (optional)

In a large skillet over medium-high heat, melt 3 tablespoons of butter; add potatoes, spreading evenly. Add spices on top. Do not disturb until crisp enough to turn, then turn and finish to desired crispness (try not to cook potatoes to "mush").

In another large skillet, cook onion and peppers in 1 tablespoon butter. Add sausage and corn; cook until heated through. Add sausage/vegetable mixture to potatoes; stir gently to mix all ingredients. Cover, lower heat to warm and cook for 20-30 minutes to marry flavors. Serve alone or with salsa.

All Seasons River Inn

During your stay at the All Seasons River Inn you can choose to relax on the comfy sofa or on your private deck overlooking the river. For a more action-packed vacation, be sure to take advantage of the seven mile bike loop that circles the city on one of the inns complimentary bicycles.

"All the warmth and simplicity of home, with all the details that make a difference. Such a wonderful getaway." ~ Guest, All Seasons River Inn

INNKEEPERS:	Kathy & Jeff Falconer
ADDRESS:	8751 Icicle Road
	Leavenworth, WA 98826
TELEPHONE:	(509) 548-1425; (800) 254-0555
E-MAIL:	info@allseasonsriverinn.com
WEBSITE:	www.allseasonsriverinn.com
ROOMS:	6 Rooms; 3 Suites; All with private baths
CHILDREN:	Children age 16 and older are welcome
ANIMALS:	Not allowed
HANDICAPPED:	Not handicapped accessible
DIETARY NEEDS:	Will accommodate guests' special dietary needs

Inspirational Hashbrowns

Makes 12 Servings

"Want to make boring hash browns more interesting? When I first began using this recipe, each preparation was a 'creation.' Just pour together whatever you have in the refrigerator, and instant rave reviews. Enjoy!" ~ Kathy Falconer, All Seasons River Inn

1   bunch green onions, chopped
1   tomato, chopped
1   cup grated cheddar cheese
1   (32-ounce) bag frozen hash browns
1   cup sour cream
1   cup cottage cheese
Salt (or garlic salt) and pepper, to taste

Preheat oven to 350°F. Mix together all ingredients in a large casserole dish. Bake, uncovered, for 1 hour. Bake a little longer for crispier hash browns.

Old Consulate Inn
(F.W. Hastings House)

Experience the gracious hospitality of the Victorian past in this beautifully restored Queen Anne masterpiece. The inn is furnished with an incredible collection of period antiques, including many pieces which were original to the mansion.

"Visit Port Townsend and the Old Consulate Inn for a trip back in time with all the comforts and luxuries of today. Come join us!" ~ Michael DeLong

INNKEEPERS:	Michael DeLong
ADDRESS:	313 Walker at Washington
	Port Townsend, WA 98368
TELEPHONE:	(360) 385-6753; (800) 300-6753
E-MAIL:	anyone@oldconsulateinn.com
WEBSITE:	www.oldconsulateinn.com
ROOMS:	8 Rooms; All with private baths
CHILDREN:	Children age 12 and older are welcome
ANIMALS:	Not allowed
HANDICAPPED:	Not handicapped accessible
DIETARY NEEDS:	Will accommodate guests' special dietary needs

Roma Romano Tomatoes

Makes 8 Side Dish Servings

12	small to medium Roma tomatoes
6	tablespoons (¾ stick) butter, melted
6	tablespoons grated Romano cheese
2	tablespoons dried basil

Preheat broiler. Using a fluting or small paring knife, cut each tomato lengthwise by making small "V" shaped cuts towards center of fruit (see *Carol's Corner* below). Place tomato halves, round-side-down, on rimmed cookie sheet or shallow baking dish. Drizzle butter into each tomato half. Sprinkle with grated cheese and a pinch of basil. Place in oven on second shelf under broiler. Broil for approximately 5 minutes, or until bubbly and browned. Serve hot.

Carol's Corner

By making V-shaped cuts to the middle of the tomato all the way around when cutting it in half, a pretty zigzag edge is formed. The resulting ridges also help keep the melted butter from running off the tomato.

Domaine Madeleine

The Ming Room at the Domaine Madeleine Bed and Breakfast occupies the entire top floor of the main house. The 30-foot balcony affords spectacular views of the Strait of Juan De Fuca and the lights of Victoria.

"A blend of Asian artistry with pampering *à la Française*. Breakfast is a visual and culinary triumph. Truly a museum-caliber B&B." ~ Guest, Domaine Madeleine

INNKEEPERS:	Jeri Weinhold
ADDRESS:	146 Wildflower Lane
	Port Angeles, WA 98362
TELEPHONE:	(360) 457-4174
E-MAIL:	romance@domainemadeleine.com
WEBSITE:	www.domainemadeleine.com
ROOMS:	1 Room; 3 Suites; 1 Cottage; All with private baths
CHILDREN:	Children age 12 and older are welcome
ANIMALS:	Not allowed
HANDICAPPED:	Not handicapped accessible
DIETARY NEEDS:	Will accommodate guests' special dietary needs

Ratatouille

Makes 6 Servings

1   pound eggplant, thinly sliced or diced
Salt and flour
½   cup olive oil, divided
1   pound zucchini, sliced
1   pound onions, thinly sliced
3   red bell peppers, roasted, peeled, seeded and cut into strips
      (or use roasted peppers that come in a jar)
5   cloves garlic, crushed
1½   pounds tomatoes, peeled, seeded and coarsely chopped
Salt and freshly ground black pepper, to taste
2   fresh thyme sprigs (or 1 teaspoon dried)
5   large fresh basil leaves, chopped (or 2-3 teaspoons dried)
Chopped fresh parsley, for garnish

Sprinkle eggplant with salt. Let stand for 20 minutes, then drain (salt will draw moisture out). Pat dry and sprinkle lightly with flour. Heat ¼ cup of olive oil in a large, heavy pan over moderate heat. Add eggplant and cook until lightly colored, stirring frequently. Add zucchini and cook for 5-6 more minutes, until lightly colored. Remove eggplant and zucchini with a slotted spoon and set aside.

Heat ¼ cup of oil. Add onions and cook until soft. Add peppers and garlic, raise heat and cook for a few minutes. Add tomatoes and cook over low heat for 10 minutes, stirring frequently. Add eggplant and zucchini; stir well to combine. Add salt and pepper. Crumble in thyme. Cook over low heat, uncovered, for 20 minutes, or until vegetables are soft, stirring occasionally. Just before serving, add basil, taste and adjust seasonings. Transfer to a warmed serving dish and sprinkle with parsley. Serve hot or cold.

> **Carol's Corner**
> *This is a versatile dish! To use as a main dish, add slices of Italian sausage. Serve ratatouille at room temperature with crackers for a nice appetizer. Make it a day in advance – it gets even better, as the flavors have a chance to blend. To use as an omelet filling, see Madeleine's creative recipe on page 133.*

St. Helens Manorhouse

Built in 1910, the St. Helens Manorhouse boasts original etched, stained and beveled glasswork. This countryside haven features beautiful woodwork and elegantly appointed guest rooms. Guests enjoy quiet walks, hiking, browsing in the antique shop or sitting by a peaceful creek.

Innkeeper Susyn Dragness was named "best breakfast cook in the Northwest" in the book *Hot Showers, Soft Beds and Dayhikes in the Central Cascades.*

INNKEEPERS:	Susyn Dragness
ADDRESS:	7476 Highway 12
	Morton, WA 98356
TELEPHONE:	(360) 498-5243; (800) 551-3290
E-MAIL:	innkeeper@myhome.net
WEBSITE:	Not available
ROOMS:	4 Rooms; All with private baths
CHILDREN:	Children age 10 and older are welcome
ANIMALS:	Call ahead
HANDICAPPED:	Call ahead
DIETARY NEEDS:	Will accommodate guests' special dietary needs

Baked Mini Pumpkins

Makes 1 Serving (Multiply as Needed)

"My guests love these, and they look so cute on the plates! They can be assembled the night before and baked in the morning." - Susyn Dragness, St. Helens Manorhouse. Be sure to use sugar pumpkins. Do not use jack o' lantern pumpkins – they are too stringy.

1   miniature sugar or pie pumpkin
1   tablespoon butter
2   tablespoons brown sugar
2   teaspoons chopped pecans, more or less
Maple syrup

Preheat oven to 300°F. Wash and dry pumpkin. Cut out top and set aside. Clean out seeds and any strings. Put butter, brown sugar and pecans into pumpkin. Put top back on pumpkin. Place pumpkin in a baking pan and pour ¼ cup water into bottom of pan. Bake for 40-50 minutes, or until tender. Remove from oven and pour a little bit of maple syrup inside pumpkin. Put top back on and serve!

Cooney Mansion

The Cooney Mansion Bed and Breakfast Inn was built in 1908 as the residence of lumber baron Neil Cooney, then manager of the Grays Harbor Commercial Company. This State and National Historic Register Landmark, with its abundance of fine woodwork, furniture and fixtures, has been restored to its original splendor.

A three-course "Lumber Baron's" breakfast is served at the massive original dining table.

INNKEEPERS:	Judi & Jim Lohr
ADDRESS:	1705 Fifth Street
	Cosmopolis, WA 98537
TELEPHONE:	(360) 533-0602
E-MAIL:	innkeeper@cooneymansion.com
WEBSITE:	www.cooneymansion.com
ROOMS:	5 Rooms; 1 Suite; All with private baths
CHILDREN:	Children age 12 and older are welcome; Call ahead
ANIMALS:	Not allowed
HANDICAPPED:	Not handicapped accessible
DIETARY NEEDS:	Call ahead

Santa Cruz Sweet and Sour Zucchini Salad

Makes 12 Servings

Start this marinated salad a day ahead to allow for full development of flavor.

¾	cup sugar
1	teaspoon salt
1	teaspoon pepper
⅓	cup salad oil
⅔	cup cider vinegar
½	cup white wine vinegar
1	cup chopped green onions (about 10 green onions)
8	cups thinly sliced zucchini (about 4-6 zucchini)
½	cup diced bell green pepper (about ½ medium pepper)
½	cup diced celery (1-2 ribs)

In a large bowl, combine sugar, salt, pepper, oil and vinegars. Add onions, zucchini, green pepper and celery. Mix well, cover and chill overnight. Drain well and serve.

✿ Carol's Corner
The marinade for this salad is great! Vary this recipe by adding whatever you have in your garden – tomatoes, red peppers, cucumbers, yellow squash, etc.

Abendblume Pension

Luxurious accommodations surround guests of the Abendblume Pension Inn. The Schnesswittchen Room offers a private balcony, heated whirlpool tub, German fireplace and European linens and comforters.

Seasonal recreational activities include downhill and cross-country skiing, sleigh rides, sledding, river rafting, bicycling, hiking, rock climbing, fishing and golf.

INNKEEPERS:	Renee Sexauer
ADDRESS:	12570 Ranger Road
	Leavenworth, WA 98826
TELEPHONE:	(509) 548-4059; (800) 669-7634
EMAIL:	abendblm@rightathome.com
WEBSITE:	www.abendblume.com
ROOMS:	7 Rooms; 4 Suites; All with private baths
CHILDREN:	Not allowed
ANIMALS:	Not allowed
HANDICAPPED:	Not handicapped accessible
DIETARY NEEDS:	Will accommodate guests' special dietary needs

Spicy Cranberry-Orange Mold

Makes 10 Servings

A nice accompaniment to Thanksgiving turkey!

1½   cups ground fresh cranberries (see substitution below)
½   cup sugar
¼   teaspoon cinnamon
⅛   teaspoon ground cloves
1   large (6-ounce) package orange-flavored gelatin
¼   teaspoon salt
2   cups boiling water
1½   cups cold water
1   tablespoon lemon juice
1   orange, peeled, sectioned and diced
½   cup chopped nuts or celery (or ¼ cup of each)
Salad greens, for garnish (optional)

In a small bowl, combine cranberries, sugar, cinnamon and cloves. Set aside. In a large bowl, dissolve gelatin and salt in boiling water. Add cold water and lemon juice. Chill gelatin mixture until slightly thickened. Fold in cranberry mixture, orange and nuts or celery. Spoon into a 6-cup ring mold (or a 6-cup capacity serving bowl). Chill until firm, about 4 hours. Unmold. Garnish with salad greens, if desired.

Substitution: In place of fresh cranberries, you can use 1 (16-ounce) can whole berry cranberry sauce. If using whole berry cranberry sauce, then omit the sugar and reduce the cold water to 1 cup.

Carol's Corner
Try this refreshing salad using your favorite flavor of gelatin. My mother tried this recipe using one 3-ounce package of apricot flavor and one 3-ounce package of mixed fruit flavor. She reported that it was delicious!

Cooney Mansion

The south lawn of the Cooney Mansion Bed and Breakfast Inn is framed by a rose garden laced with clematis, lilacs and peonies. The north lawn features a rhododendron grove and a sprawling lawn surrounded by pine forest.

Cooney Mansion hosts "A Dickens Family Christmas" the first two weeks in December, featuring high tea with Queen Victoria, arts, crafts and Victorian dinners.

INNKEEPERS:	Judi & Jim Lohr
ADDRESS:	1705 Fifth Street
	Cosmopolis, WA 98537
TELEPHONE:	(360) 533-0602
E-MAIL:	innkeeper@cooneymansion.com
WEBSITE:	www.cooneymansion.com
ROOMS:	5 Rooms; 1 Suite; All with private baths
CHILDREN:	Children age 12 and older are welcome; Call ahead
ANIMALS:	Not allowed
HANDICAPPED:	Not handicapped accessible
DIETARY NEEDS:	Call ahead

Judi's Chinese Chicken Salad

Makes 6 Entrée Servings or 12 Side-Dish Servings

Start this recipe several hours before serving to allow time to chill the salad. The marinated chicken adds great flavor to the salad!

2	tablespoons sugar
1	teaspoon salt
1	tablespoon vinegar
2	tablespoons soy sauce
¼	teaspoon ground ginger
1	clove garlic, minced
½	cup salad oil
½	teaspoon white pepper
¼	cup lemon juice
1	cup shredded cooked chicken
½	head cabbage, shredded
½	head iceberg lettuce, shredded
1	bunch green onions, sliced
2	tablespoons sesame seeds, lightly toasted
2	tablespoons slivered almonds or chopped salted peanuts
½	package uncooked ramen noodles, crumbled
½	small bunch fresh cilantro, chopped

In a medium bowl, mix sugar, salt, vinegar, soy sauce, ginger, garlic, oil, white pepper and lemon juice. Add cooked chicken, coating thoroughly with dressing. Marinate in the refrigerator for several hours.

Approximately 15-20 minutes before serving, in a large bowl, combine cabbage, lettuce, green onions, sesame seeds, almonds, ramen noodles and cilantro. Add chicken and dressing. Toss together and serve.

Luncheon & Dinner Entrées

Luncheon

&

Dinner

Entrées

Benson Farmstead

The Benson Farmstead Bed and Breakfast is a cozy farmhouse that was lovingly restored in 1981 by Jerry and Sharon Benson, grandchildren of Skagit Valley Norwegian pioneers. This 17 room house is filled with lovely antiques, Scandinavian curios and old quilts.

"A little bit of heaven on earth." ~ Guest, Benson Farmstead

INNKEEPERS:	Jerry & Sharon Benson
ADDRESS:	10113 Avon-Allen Road
	Bow, WA 98232
TELEPHONE:	(360) 757-0578; (800) 441-9814
E-MAIL:	bensonfarmstead@hotmail.com
WEBSITE:	www.bbhost.com/bensonbnb
ROOMS:	4 Rooms; 2 Cottages; All with private baths
CHILDREN:	Welcome
ANIMALS:	Not allowed
HANDICAPPED:	Not handicapped accessible
DIETARY NEEDS:	Will accommodate guests' special dietary needs

Benson's Luncheon Chicken Casserole

Makes 8 Servings

Great with cranberries, a salad and rolls!

7	boneless skinless chicken breast halves
1	small onion, quartered
2	ribs celery, cut in several pieces
1	teaspoon Johnny's Pork & Chicken Seasoning (very flavorful seasoned salt), or other seasoned salt
1	(10¾-ounce) can cream of mushroom soup
1	pint sour cream
½	pound fresh mushrooms, sliced and sautéed
½	stick (¼ cup) butter or margarine, melted
1	cup chicken stock (reserved from cooking chicken)
1	(8-ounce) package Pepperidge Farm herb seasoned or cornbread stuffing mix

Put chicken, onion and celery into a large saucepan; add enough water to cover. Simmer for 20 minutes, or until cooked. Remove chicken and strain cooking liquid, reserving 1 cup of cooking liquid. Cut chicken into chunks.

Preheat oven to 325°F. Coat a 13x9-inch baking dish with nonstick cooking spray. Place chicken in bottom of dish and sprinkle with seasoned salt. Cover with soup, then sour cream, then mushrooms. In a large bowl, combine melted butter and the 1 cup reserved chicken cooking liquid; toss with stuffing mix and spread over top of ingredients in dish. Bake, uncovered, for 50 minutes.

Seven C's Guest Ranch

The 7 C's (Seven Seas) Guest Ranch Bed and Breakfast is a ten-acre farm that combines modern luxury with country comfort. After a peaceful night's rest, guests enjoy a delicious farm breakfast. Gourmet meals can be arranged in advance.

Special amenities include horseback riding, overnight stabling, hay rides or an outdoor hot spa that can accommodate seven.

INNKEEPERS:	Evelyn B. Cissna
ADDRESS:	11123 128th SE
	Rainier, WA 98576
TELEPHONE:	(360) 446-7957
E-MAIL:	Not available
WEBSITE:	Not available
ROOMS:	4 Rooms; 1 Suite; Private and shared baths
CHILDREN:	Welcome
ANIMALS:	Permitted outside only
HANDICAPPED:	Is handicapped accessible
DIETARY NEEDS:	Will accommodate guests' special dietary needs

Reception Turkey Salad

Makes 12 Servings

This tasty salad is perfect for any occasion or celebration, from a neighborhood potluck or baby shower, to a wedding reception! This recipe needs to be made at least several hours in advance to allow the flavors to marry.

3	cups cubed cooked turkey or chicken
½	(8-ounce) can pineapple tidbits, drained (reserve juice for dressing)
½	(11-ounce) can mandarin orange segments, drained
½	cup red or green grapes, halved
½	cup chopped apples
½	cup chopped celery
3	tablespoons slivered or chopped sweet pickles
4	hard-cooked eggs, chopped
½	cup chopped cashews

Dressing:

1	cup Best Foods or Hellman's mayonnaise (don't substitute)
2	tablespoons lemon juice
2	tablespoons pineapple juice (from drained pineapple tidbits)
½	teaspoon grated lemon zest
1	teaspoon salt

In a very large bowl, combine turkey or chicken, pineapple, mandarin oranges, grapes, apples, celery, pickles and eggs. Set aside.

In a medium bowl, combine mayonnaise, lemon juice, 2 tablespoons reserved pineapple juice, lemon zest and salt. Pour over turkey/fruit mixture and stir gently to thoroughly combine. Refrigerate for several hours (if possible) to marry the flavors. Add cashews just before serving.

Make-ahead tip: Salad may be made 1 day in advance, but remember to stir in cashews just before serving.

Moby Dick Hotel & Oyster Farm

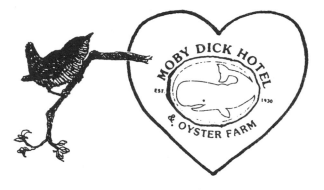

The Moby Dick Hotel and Oyster Farm was built in 1929 as a hotel. During World War II, this historic dwelling was headquarters to the United States Coast Guard Horse Patrol which patrolled the ocean beaches.

The spacious public rooms and rambling bay-front grounds provide an ideal setting for small focus groups, staff retreats or family reunions.

INNKEEPERS:	Fritzi Cohen
ADDRESS:	Sandridge Road; PO Box 82
	Nahcotta, WA 98637
TELEPHONE:	(360) 665-4543
E-MAIL:	mobydickhotel@willapabay.org
WEBSITE:	www.mobydickhotel.com
ROOMS:	8 Rooms; Shared baths
CHILDREN:	Welcome
ANIMALS:	Dogs welcome
HANDICAPPED:	Call ahead
DIETARY NEEDS:	Call ahead

Moby Dick Oysters

Makes As Many Servings As You Wish

Looking for an unusual and impressive appetizer? Here it is! "This is Moby Dick's version of Oysters Rockefeller. We serve it at dinner or as a garnish at breakfast with oyster breakfast dishes that we make." ~ Fritzi Cohen, Moby Dick Hotel & Oyster Farm

Oysters in the shell (2-3 per person for an appetizer)
Mustard greens, kale or arugula
Aioli (recipe follows)
Parmesan cheese, grated

Preheat oven to 500°F or preheat broiler. Shuck or steam oysters open. Save shell halves that are the most attractive and stable. Finely chiffonade (cut into thin strips or shreds) the greens and put a bit into each shell. Put an oyster back into each shell on top of the greens. Put a bit of greens on top of each oyster. Top with a dab of aioli. Sprinkle with Parmesan cheese and put them in the oven or under the broiler until aioli browns very slightly.

Aioli:
2-3 cloves garlic, or more to taste
Handful of fresh herbs (basil and cilantro are good)
1   teaspoon salt
1   whole egg
1   egg yolk
Lemon or lime juice or various vinegars, to your taste (start with at least 1 generous tablespoon)
1¼   cups any good oil (Fritzi uses a mix of olive and corn oils)

Process garlic, herbs and salt in a food processor or blender. Add egg and egg yolk, lemon or lime juice or vinegars and process briefly. While processor is running, slowly dribble in oil until mixture is thickened (add more oil if needed). Keep any leftover aioli refrigerated.

Selah Inn

Nestled on the north shore of the Hood Canal, Selah Inn on Dulalip Landing offers guests a memorable and relaxing experience. The living room of this elegant Northwest lodge is dominated by a magnificent rock fireplace. Amenities include luxurious linens, fresh flowers and chocolates.

Conference facilities for small business meetings are available by prior arrangement. White board, overhead and computer hookups are provided.

INNKEEPERS:	Pat & Bonnie McCullough
ADDRESS:	130 NE Dulalip Landing
	Belfair, WA 98528
TELEPHONE:	(360) 275-0916; (360) 275-0578
E-MAIL:	innkeeper@selahinn.com
WEBSITE:	www.selahinn.com
ROOMS:	4 Rooms; 1 Suite; 5 Cottages; Private and shared baths
CHILDREN:	Welcome in cottages only
ANIMALS:	Not allowed
HANDICAPPED:	Call ahead
DIETARY NEEDS:	Will accommodate guests' special dietary needs

Champagne Poached Oysters with Brie Sauce

Makes 8 Appetizer Servings or 4 Entrée Servings

2	dozen clean oyster shells
1	(10-ounce) package chopped spinach, steamed and drained
1	cup champagne or sparkling wine
½	teaspoon saffron
½	teaspoon dried basil
1	pinch cayenne
1	quart shucked oysters (reserve oyster liquid)
½	cup sour cream
½	cup heavy cream
8	ounces Brie cheese, rind removed and cut into 1-inch squares

Parsley, for garnish

Preheat oven to 175°F. Fill each clean oyster shell with 1 tablespoon cooked spinach. Place shells on a baking sheet and keep warm in oven.

In a large pan, bring wine, saffron, basil and cayenne to a simmer. Add oysters and reserved liquid. Poach oysters until plump and firm, about 3 minutes. With slotted spoon, remove oysters and place atop spinach in individual shells; keep warm in oven.

Boil remaining liquid until reduced to ¼ cup. Beat together sour cream and heavy cream. Stir into reduced liquid and heat until mixture begins to bubble. Add chunks of Brie. Whisk until cheese melts and sauce thickens. Pour over warm oysters, garnish with parsley and serve immediately.

Note: You may omit the oyster shells and spinach and serve the oysters with the sauce only.

S ince 1907, The Captain Whidbey Inn has provided travelers with warm hospitality, wonderful food and comfortable rooms furnished with antiques, artwork, books, down comforters and feather beds.

Guests enjoy dining on world famous Penn Cove mussels, steelhead salmon, Dungeness crab or spot prawns, all provided by local fishermen to ensure peak freshness.

INNKEEPERS:	John C. Stone & Mandy McLean-Stone
ADDRESS:	2072 West Captain Whidbey Inn Road
	Coupeville, Whidbey Island, WA 98239
TELEPHONE:	(360) 678-4097; (800) 366-4097
E-MAIL:	info@captainwhidbey.com
WEBSITE:	www.captainwhidbey.com
ROOMS:	25 Rooms; 7 Cabins; Private and shared baths
CHILDREN:	Welcome
ANIMALS:	Not allowed
HANDICAPPED:	Cabins are handicapped accessible
DIETARY NEEDS:	Will accommodate guests' special dietary needs

Ginger Mussels

Makes 2 Appetizer Servings or 1 Entrée Serving

A frequently requested recipe at The Captain Whidbey Inn.

1   pound (about 18-20) mussels, cleaned and de-bearded
1   cup Ginger Mussel Mix (recipe follows)

Place mussels into a hot skillet. Add Ginger Mussel Mix and cover. Cook until mussels open, about 3-5 minutes (discard any mussels that do not open). Transfer mussels and broth to bowl; serve immediately.

Ginger Mussel Mix:

2½   teaspoons minced fresh ginger
⅓   cup finely chopped green onions (about ½ bunch)
1   small clove garlic, minced
¾   teaspoon black pepper
1-2   jalapeño peppers, seeds and membranes removed, minced
1   tablespoon sesame oil
¼   cup plus ½ tablespoon rice vinegar
2   tablespoons soy sauce
½   cup plus ½ tablespoon sake (Japanese rice wine)

Combine all ingredients. Store in refrigerator. Stir well before using.

Carol's Corner

Wash your hands thoroughly after removing the seeds and membranes from the jalapeño peppers (or wear rubber gloves). Otherwise, the oils from the peppers can cause a burning sensation to your eyes if you accidentally touch them. If this should happen, immediately flush your eyes with water.

Inn at Barnum Point

The Inn at Barnum Point is a birdwatcher's haven. Guests observe magnificent soaring eagles, diminutive hummingbirds, flocks of Dunlin or happy goldfinch munching on cherries.

Animal lovers discover seals and otters playing in the water, deer grazing in the orchard or hear coyotes howling in the night.

INNKEEPERS:	Carolin Barnum Dilorenzo
ADDRESS:	464 South Barnum Road
	Camano Island, WA 98292
TELEPHONE:	(360) 387-2256; (800) 910-2256
E-MAIL:	barnum@camano.net
WEBSITE:	www.innatbarnumpoint.com
ROOMS:	3 Rooms; All with private baths
CHILDREN:	Welcome
ANIMALS:	Not allowed
HANDICAPPED:	Not handicapped accessible
DIETARY NEEDS:	Will accommodate guests' special dietary needs

Salmon with Blackberry Sauce

Makes 4 Servings

2   cups blackberries, divided (or frozen, thawed)
¼   cup sugar
¼   cup water
¼   cup red wine vinegar
½   tablespoon butter
¼   cup minced onions or shallots
¼   cup dry red wine
Salt and pepper, to taste
4   salmon fillets (about ½-pound each), skinned
¼   teaspoon ground cloves
3   tablespoons fresh thyme leaves, plus a few sprigs for garnish
1½   tablespoons salad oil

In a food processor or blender, purée 1½ cups blackberries. Pass berries through a fine sieve, using back of spoon to help push purée through; set aside. In a small saucepan, mix sugar and water. Cook over medium-high heat until reduced to a thick, light, caramel-colored syrup, about 5-10 minutes. Remove from heat. Add vinegar, return to low heat and stir until thoroughly combined.

In a small saucepan, melt butter over medium-high heat. Add onions and cook, stirring often, until just golden brown. Add wine and cook until most of liquid evaporates, 5-10 minutes – watch carefully. Add berry purée and cook until reduced by half, 6-10 minutes. Add half of vinegar/syrup mixture (or more to taste). Season with salt and pepper. Set aside.

Rinse salmon; pat dry. Season with salt and pepper. Sprinkle cloves and thyme on a plate. Dip salmon in this mixture, turning to coat each side. Preheat oven to 375°F. Heat oil in a large ovenproof skillet over high heat. Add salmon and cook until lightly browned, 1-2 minutes per side. Transfer to oven and bake for 4-6 minutes, or until barely opaque in thickest part. While salmon cooks, add remaining ½ cup of blackberries to sauce and heat through over medium heat.

To serve: Spoon sauce onto 4 serving plates and place a salmon fillet on top. Garnish with sprigs of thyme and whole berries.

Selah Inn

The spectacular Northwest wonderland of the Hood Canal awaits guests of the Selah Inn. The Hood Canal, a 60-mile extension of Puget Sound, is a haven for wildlife. Beach walks are a great opportunity to observe eagles, cranes, gulls, ducks and sea lions.

McCormick Woods and Gold Mountain golf courses are within 10 miles of the inn. Bike trails and off-road recreational vehicle trails abound in a local off-road recreational park.

INNKEEPERS:	Pat & Bonnie McCullough
ADDRESS:	130 NE Dulalip Landing
	Belfair, WA 98528
TELEPHONE:	(360) 275-0916; (877) 232-7941
E-MAIL:	innkeeper@selahinn.com
WEBSITE:	www.selahinn.com
ROOMS:	4 Rooms; 1 Suite; 2 Cottage; Private and shared baths
CHILDREN:	Welcome in cottages only
ANIMALS:	Not allowed
HANDICAPPED:	Call ahead
DIETARY NEEDS:	Will accommodate guests' special dietary needs

Salmon with Roasted Garlic and Sun-Dried Tomato Herb Butter

Makes 4 Servings

Make-ahead tip: The roasted garlic and sun-dried tomato herb butter may be made in advance and stored in the refrigerator until one hour before using.

1   bulb garlic
4   tablespoons olive oil, divided
⅓   cup sun-dried tomatoes (soaked in water and drained) or oil-packed sun-dried tomatoes (drained)
1   stick (½ cup) butter
1   teaspoon dried rosemary
2   pounds boneless, skinless salmon fillet
Old Bay seasoning (for seafood, poultry and meats)
Fresh dill, for garnish
Lemon wedges, for garnish

For roasted garlic: Preheat oven to 350°F. With a sharp knife, cut about ¼-inch off top of garlic bulb (leave paper-like skin on to hold cloves together). On a small sheet of foil, pour 1 tablespoon of olive oil. Place garlic bulb cut-side-down on oil; wrap foil around bulb. Bake for 45-60 minutes, until cloves are very soft. Cool, then gently squeeze out garlic cloves into bowl of food processor.

In food processor, blend roasted garlic, 3 tablespoons olive oil, sun-dried tomatoes, butter and rosemary. (This may be made in advance and stored in refrigerator until 1 hour before using.)

Raise oven temperature to 425°F. Cover a baking sheet with foil. Rinse salmon with cold water, pat dry and put on baking sheet. Sprinkle salmon with Old Bay seasoning. Spread roasted garlic/butter mixture evenly over top of salmon. Bake for 10-12 minutes, checking occasionally for doneness by inserting a knife into the thickest part and gently parting flesh – salmon is done when just opaque throughout (do not overcook). Slice into serving portions. Serve immediately, garnished with fresh dill and lemon wedges.

The Captain Whidbey Inn

I nnkeeper John Colby Stone is a sailing charter captain. Guests of The Captain Whidbey Inn often book an afternoon on his 52 foot classic wooden ketch, Cutty Sark. Captain Stone encourages his guests to take a turn at the helm, help trim the sails or simply enjoy the cruise with its splendid views of the water, islands and mountains.

The Inn's charming dining room overlooks the beautiful waters of Penn Cove.

INNKEEPERS:	John C. Stone & Mandy McLean-Stone
ADDRESS:	2072 West Captain Whidbey Inn Road
	Coupeville, Whidbey Island, WA 98239
TELEPHONE:	(360) 678-4097; (800) 366-4097
E-MAIL:	info@captainwhidbey.com
WEBSITE:	www.captainwhidbey.com
ROOMS:	25 Rooms; 7 Cabins; Private and shared baths
CHILDREN:	Welcome
ANIMALS:	Not allowed
HANDICAPPED:	Cabins are handicapped accessible
DIETARY NEEDS:	Will accommodate guests' special dietary needs

Sesame-Crusted Halibut with Lemon Sage Butter

Makes 4 Servings

"Native Americans used wood to barbecue fish over open fire pits. It flavors the fish with a hint of charred wood and helps keep the flesh tender. Untreated alder, hickory, cherry or cedar planks work well." - The Captain Whidbey Inn

1   stick (½ cup) butter, room temperature
½   tablespoon chopped fresh sage leaves
½   tablespoon minced garlic
Juice and grated zest of ¼ lemon
½   cup milk
1   cup sesame seeds
½   cup flour
Salt and white pepper, to taste
4   halibut fillets (about 4 ounces each)
2-3 tablespoons olive oil, divided
Wood plank for baking fish (see note above and *Carol's Corner* below)

For the lemon sage butter: In a medium bowl, whip butter, sage, garlic, lemon juice and lemon zest with an electric mixer until fluffy. Shape into a 3-inch log and wrap in waxed paper. Chill until butter is firm.

Preheat oven to 425°F. In a shallow dish, pour milk. In another shallow dish, combine sesame seeds, flour, salt and white pepper. Dip fish into milk, then into sesame seed mixture, turning to lightly coat each side. In 2 medium, nonstick skillets, heat 1 tablespoon of oil until it just begins to smoke. Add 2 halibut fillets to each pan and brown each side, about 1 minute per side. Put fish on wood plank; bake for 10-15 minutes, or until flesh feels firm to the touch. Top each fillet with 1 tablespoon of lemon sage butter and serve.

> *Carol's Corner*
> *Many kitchen stores sell beautiful wood planks designed for baking. Or purchase less expensive, rustic boards at home improvement stores (do not use pressure treated wood).*

The Manor Farm Inn

The Manor Farm Inn offers guests an oasis of tranquillity and seclusion. Its 25 pastoral acres boast a century-old farmhouse, and porches and verandah posts framed by delicate climbing rose vines and a happy profusion of seasonal flowers.

The decor is unpretentiously lovely with country French pine antiques, colorful flower baskets and cozy firelit nooks.

INNKEEPERS:	Janet Plemmons
ADDRESS:	26069 Big Valley Road NE
	Poulsbo, WA 98370
TELEPHONE:	(360) 779-4628
E-MAIL:	information@manorfarminn.com
WEBSITE:	www.manorfarminn.com
ROOMS:	6 Rooms; All with private baths
CHILDREN:	Children age 16 and older are welcome
ANIMALS:	Not allowed
HANDICAPPED:	Not handicapped accessible
DIETARY NEEDS:	Will accommodate guests' special dietary needs

Balsamic and Beer-Braised Lamb with Rosemary White Beans

Makes 4 to 6 Servings

Ask your butcher to cut the meat off the bone and into cubes. Save the bone, it will add flavor to the beans. Start this recipe the day before, as the beans need to soak overnight. If you are short on time, substitute 3 cups drained, canned white beans.

Beans:

1½   cups white beans, soaked in water overnight and drained
2   (14½-ounce) cans vegetable broth
1   lamb bone (optional)
Salt and pepper, to taste
1½   teaspoons chopped fresh rosemary
1   head garlic, roasted (see page 221)

In a large pot, cover soaked and drained beans with vegetable broth. Add lamb bone, if desired. Bring to a boil, cover, lower heat and simmer until tender, about 1 hour. Season with salt, pepper and rosemary. Squeeze roasted garlic cloves into beans; mix gently. Keep warm until serving.

Lamb:

3   tablespoons olive oil, divided
2   pounds leg of lamb, cut into 1-inch cubes
1   small onion, thinly sliced
1   (12-ounce) bottle beer
1   cup balsamic vinegar
1   cup stock (preferably lamb stock)
2   tablespoons cornstarch mixed with 2 tablespoons water

In a large skillet over high heat, heat 2 tablespoons oil and sear lamb in batches, browning evenly on all sides. Remove lamb and set aside. Add 1 tablespoon oil to skillet and slowly, lightly brown onions. Deglaze pan with beer; add vinegar and stock. Return lamb to pan. Bring to a simmer. Cover and cook lamb gently for 1-1½ hours, or until tender. Add cornstarch mixture and stir until thickened. Serve over or around the beans.

The Willows Inn

Set against a backdrop of colorful rhododendrons and towering evergreens, The Willows Inn Bed and Breakfast is an island retreat where guests enjoy spectacular sunsets over the Gulf Islands. Situated on Lummi, this wooded, rural island is graced with tranquil beaches and 18 miles of country roads ideal for biking, bird watching or hiking.

The inn offers complete wedding services, including ceremony, reception and honeymoon.

INNKEEPERS:	Judy & Riley Stark
ADDRESS:	2579 West Shore Drive
	Lummi Island, WA 98262
TELEPHONE:	(360) 758-2620
E-MAIL:	willows@willows-inn.com
WEBSITE:	www.willows-inn.com
ROOMS:	7 Rooms; 2 Suites; 1 Cottage; All with private baths
CHILDREN:	Children age 8 and older are welcome; call ahead
ANIMALS:	Not allowed
HANDICAPPED:	Is handicapped accessible
DIETARY NEEDS:	Will accommodate guests' special dietary needs

Herbed Lamb Chops

Makes 1 Serving (Multiply as Needed)

Ellensburg lamb chops come from a quaint college town in Central Washington known for its tender, succulent lamb. This recipe is easy and elegant, but you do have to plan ahead.

2   thick double Ellensburg lamb chops
1   tablespoon chopped fresh rosemary
1   tablespoon chopped fresh thyme
1   tablespoon chopped fresh sage
1   tablespoon dried Italian seasoning
2   garlic cloves, minced
Olive oil
3   fresh rosemary branches

Twenty-four hours ahead, trim all fat from lamb chops. In a small bowl, make dry marinade by mixing together rosemary, thyme, sage, Italian seasoning and garlic. Lightly coat a glass dish or pan with olive oil and sprinkle in some of dry marinade. Place chops on mixture and rub with more olive oil and dry marinade. Place a couple rosemary branches on top, cover and refrigerate overnight.

Prior to cooking, bring chops to room temperature. Preheat grill. Grill chops for 4 minutes on first side and 3 minutes on other side, or to desired doneness (lamb is good served medium-rare – be careful not to overcook it). Remove chops to a warm plate and let rest for at least 5 minutes. Garnish with a fresh rosemary branch.

> 🌿 *Carol's Corner*
> *This special recipe was served at a winemaker's dinner featuring the Chinook Winery in 1994. The innkeepers at The Willows Inn suggest accompanying the lamb chops with minted and buttered tiny red potatoes, honeyed baby carrots, steamed asparagus topped with chopped, toasted hazelnuts and a bottle of Chinook Merlot.*

A Touch of Europe

Situated on one acre of maple, pine, birch, cedar and spruce trees, and surrounded by an array of beautiful flowers, A Touch of Europe Bed and Breakfast Inn invites guests to enjoy a true Victorian atmosphere enriched with old-world European charm and hospitality.

Guests complement their stay by visiting local wineries, antique shops and museums, or strolling, biking and jogging along Yakima's Greenway Path.

INNKEEPERS:	Erika G. & James A. Cenci
ADDRESS:	220 North 16th Avenue
	Yakima, WA 98902
TELEPHONE:	(509) 454-9775; (888) 438-7073
E-MAIL:	atoeurope@msn.com
WEBSITE:	www.winesnw.com/toucheuropeb&b.htm
ROOMS:	3 Rooms; All with private baths
CHILDREN:	Not allowed
ANIMALS:	Not allowed
HANDICAPPED:	Not handicapped accessible
DIETARY NEEDS:	Will accommodate guests' special dietary needs

Signature Medallions of Pork Tenderloin in a Pink Peppercorn-Riesling Sauce

Makes 4 to 6 Servings

2   tablespoons unsalted butter
1   teaspoon olive oil
1½-2 pounds pork tenderloin, cut into ½-inch slices
2   shallots, peeled and chopped
Sea salt and black pepper, to taste
½   cup dry Riesling wine
1   cup heavy cream
1   teaspoon whole pink peppercorns
½   cup sour cream
1   tablespoon chopped fresh parsley, for garnish

In a medium skillet, heat butter and oil. Brown pork slices in small batches. Remove to a plate as they finish cooking; keep warm by covering with foil.

In the same pan, gently cook shallots until soft. Return meat to pan and add salt and pepper. Stir in wine and cook for 5 minutes. Stir in cream and simmer for 15 more minutes. Add pink peppercorns and sour cream. Stir over low heat until sauce is smooth. Place several pork medallions on each serving plate. Top with a spoonful of sauce and garnish with parsley.

> ### Carol's Corner
> *The pink peppercorns in this delightful sauce add flavor and also a colorful touch. Pink peppercorns are not true peppercorns, but are actually freeze-dried berries from a rose plant cultivated in Madagascar. The berries are pungent and slightly sweet, and can usually be found in gourmet stores.*

Mountain Home Lodge

Secluded in its own alpine valley, Mountain Home Lodge overlooks a 20 acre meadow with the grandeur of the Stuart Range in the background. This sheltered hideaway offers one of the Northwest's most spectacular settings for relaxation and adventure.

During winter, access to this private lodge is provided by snowcat. Guests enjoy cross-country skiing, snowmobiling or frolicking on the 1,700-foot sledding hill.

INNKEEPERS:	Brad & Kathy Schmidt
ADDRESS:	8201 Mountain Home Road
	Leavenworth, WA 98826
TELEPHONE:	(509) 548-7077; (800) 414-2378
E-MAIL:	info@mthome.com
WEBSITE:	www.mthome.com
ROOMS:	9 Rooms; 1 Suite; 2 Cabins; All with private baths
CHILDREN:	Call ahead
ANIMALS:	Not allowed
HANDICAPPED:	Not handicapped accessible
DIETARY NEEDS:	Will accommodate guests' special dietary needs

Duck with Marionberry Compote

Makes 6 to 8 Servings

*A delicious Northwest berry sauce to serve with duck or chicken. Plan ahead —
the poultry marinates for 1 to 2 hours, then cooks for 2 hours in a smoker.
Home smokers are very popular these days and can be purchased at most major
discount chains and wholesale clubs, as well as cookware and hardware stores.*

1	cup soy sauce
1	cup sugar
1	teaspoon ground ginger
1	teaspoon minced garlic
4	cups water
4	whole boneless duck or chicken breasts (about 3 pounds)

Marionberry compote (recipe follows)

In a large bowl, thoroughly combine soy sauce, sugar, ginger, garlic and
water. Add duck or chicken breasts and marinate for 1-2 hours in refrigerator. Remove meat from marinade (discard marinade) and smoke meat for
about 2 hours, adjusting smoking time to your smoker. Slice meat thinly
on the diagonal. Serve with marionberry compote.

Marionberry compote:

2	cups marionberries (or other blackberries)
1	teaspoon cinnamon
2	cups sugar
⅓	cup balsamic vinegar

In a large saucepan, combine berries, cinnamon, sugar and vinegar. Cook
over medium-low heat until thickened, approximately 2 hours. Set aside to
cool slightly (it will thicken a bit). Sauce should be served warm. Compote
can be served under the meat or alongside it.

Make-ahead tip: Compote can be made a day or two ahead and refrigerated.
Reheat on stovetop or microwave. Thin with a little water, if necessary.

B & B Potpourri

B&B Potpourri

Island Escape

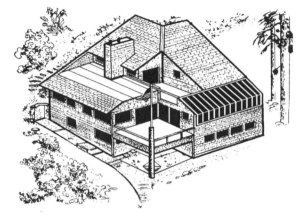

Recessed lighting sets the tone for a romantic getaway at Island Escape Bed and Breakfast. This singular suite features a private entrance, deck, garden area and a hammock built for two, with spectacular views of the Olympic Mountains.

Amenities include fresh flowers, bedside chocolates, fluffy towels and robes, herbal bath grains, oatmeal shell hand soaps and a bottle of sparkling cider upon arrival.

INNKEEPERS:	Paula E. Pascoe
ADDRESS:	210 Island Boulevard
	Fox Island, WA 98333
TELEPHONE:	(253) 549-2044; (877) 549-2044
E-MAIL:	paula@island-escape.com
WEBSITE:	www.island-escape.com
ROOMS:	1 Executive Suite; Private bath
CHILDREN:	Welcome
ANIMALS:	Call ahead
HANDICAPPED:	Not handicapped accessible
DIETARY NEEDS:	Will accommodate guests' special dietary needs

Island Escape's Orange Smoothies

Makes 2 to 3 Servings (About 3 cups)

"I cut peeled bananas into chunks, then freeze them in plastic freezer bags; they hold for nearly 2 weeks without turning brown. To make the orange smoothie heartier during winter months, I add three or four chunks of frozen banana to my smoothies. The frozen chunks slice easily and I only add a slice at a time so that it blends well with the rest of the mixture." ~ Paula Pascoe, Island Escape

2 **cups orange juice**
½ **cup plain non-fat yogurt**
2 **tablespoons sugar**
1 **cup crushed ice**
Fresh mint sprigs, for garnish

In a blender, mix together all ingredients, except mint. Serve in pre-chilled glasses. Top with your favorite mint sprig (Paula at the Island Escape rotates between her backyard mints – orange, apple and chocolate).

Run of the River

Run of the River Bed and Breakfast is the perfect getaway to enjoy mountains, streams, wildflowers and waterfalls. This natural log inn features expansive views of the spectacular Icicle River and the Cascade Mountains.

Guest rooms offer hand-hewn log furniture, spacious decks and easy access to a hot tub overlooking the river.

INNKEEPERS:	Monty & Karen Turner
ADDRESS:	9308 East Leavenworth Road
	Leavenworth, WA 98826
TELEPHONE:	(509) 548-7171; (800) 288-6491
E-MAIL:	info@runoftheriver.com
WEBSITE:	www.runoftheriver.com
ROOMS:	6 Rooms; All with private baths
CHILDREN:	Not allowed
ANIMALS:	Not allowed
HANDICAPPED:	Is handicapped accessible
DIETARY NEEDS:	Will accommodate guests' special dietary needs

Boat Drinks

Makes 6 cups Each (see next page for more Boat Drinks)

"These 'boat drinks' can be added to or altered to suit individual tastes. The secret is to use the freshest local ingredients. In summer, the blueberry, raspberry, strawberry and peach smoothies are wonderful. In fall, winter and spring, we serve Pure Gold with Golden Delicious apples (see page 239). Guests enjoy the fresh tastes of Washington and Wenatchee Valley. Boat drinks are the most 'asked for' breakfast recipe we serve. Maybe we should change the menu? 'Boat drinks' is a take-off from a Jimmy Buffett tune. You don't have to love Buffett to enjoy these drinks, but it helps." ~ Monty Turner, Run of the River

Razzmatazz:
2	cups raspberries
1½	cups raspberry yogurt
1	banana
1	tablespoon wheat bran
3	cups Woodring Orchards Apple Cider

Whirl all ingredients in blender until smooth.

Blue Wave:
2	cups blueberries
1½	cups blueberry yogurt
1	banana
2	tablespoons molasses
3	cups Woodring Orchards Apple Cider
1	tablespoon flax seeds (available at natural food stores)

Whirl all ingredients in blender until smooth.

Carol's Corner

Woodring Orchards Apple Cider is a non-pasteurized cider made in Cashmere, Washington. It is available at fruit stands throughout the valley and at Pike Place Market in Seattle. If this cider is not available in your area, substitute any good "country style," unfiltered cider.

Run of the River

S et in Washington's Cascade Range, Run of the River Bed and Breakfast offers guests a chance to connect with nature and experience the simple beauty of four seasons in the country.

"People who come here like to hike and bike and explore. They come for sun-filled, mountain-filled days. It's a beautiful place where you can do nothing but sit and read. It's also a wonderful area for getting out and connecting with nature." ~ Owners, Run of the River

INNKEEPERS:	Monty & Karen Turner
ADDRESS:	9308 East Leavenworth Road
	Leavenworth, WA 98826
TELEPHONE:	(509) 548-7171; (800) 288-6491
E-MAIL:	info@runoftheriver.com
WEBSITE:	www.runoftheriver.com
ROOMS:	6 Rooms; All with private baths
CHILDREN:	Not allowed
ANIMALS:	Not allowed
HANDICAPPED:	Is handicapped accessible
DIETARY NEEDS:	Will accommodate guests' special dietary needs

More Boat Drinks!

Makes 6 cups Each

These breakfast smoothies are not only great tasting, but they are also good for you! The yogurt (Run of the River uses low-fat or non-fat) raises the calcium and protein content, and the bran, seeds and fruit add fiber. Drink up!

Pure Gold:

1   large Golden Delicious apple, cubed (peeled or unpeeled)
1   banana
1   tablespoon chopped almonds
1½   cups vanilla yogurt
3   cups Woodring Orchards Apple Cider

Whirl all ingredients in blender until smooth.

The Berries and the Bees:

2   cups strawberries
1   banana
1   tablespoon bee pollen (available at health food stores)
1½   cups strawberry yogurt
3   cups Woodring Orchards Apple Cider

Whirl all ingredients in blender until smooth.

You're a Peach:

2   medium unpeeled peaches, sliced
1   banana
1   tablespoon chopped pecans
1½   cups peach yogurt
3   cups Woodring Orchards Apple Cider

Whirl all ingredients in blender until smooth.

> **Carol's Corner**
> *We were served a Berries and the Bees Boat Drink at Run of the River. The delicious drink gave us energy to try snowshoeing for the first time! Run of the River offers free snowshoes to their guests.*

Country Inn Guest House

L ocated on a working farm and cattle ranch in the Palouse Hills of eastern Washington State, the Country Inn Guest House is less than a mile from the old Milwaukee Railroad Corridor, also known as the John Wayne Trail.

Innkeeper Kent is a third generation owner of this 100-year-old homestead. Innkeeper Jeanne gives historical tours that include the oldest consecrated church in Washington.

INNKEEPERS:	Kent & Jeanne Kjack
ADDRESS:	1402 Cache Creek Road
	Rosalia, WA 99170
TELEPHONE:	(509) 569-3312
E-MAIL:	sasysissy@webtv.net
WEBSITE:	www.bnbweb.com/country-inn.html
ROOMS:	1 Suite; Private bath
CHILDREN:	Welcome
ANIMALS:	Welcome (must be leashed)
HANDICAPPED:	Is handicapped accessible
DIETARY NEEDS:	Cannot accommodate guests' special dietary needs

Smoked Salmon Roll-Ups

Makes 50-60 Bite-size Appetizers

"I have made these salmon logs ahead, frozen them in plastic bags, then thawed and sliced them for guests. For the pâté, any smoked fish can be used, but I think salmon is best." ~ Jeanne Kjack, Country Inn Guest Ranch

½   pound smoked salmon, flaked or mashed with a fork
     (remove any bones first)
Mayonnaise (enough to bind the salmon, start with ½ cup)
1-3 tablespoons finely chopped celery
1-3 tablespoons finely chopped onion or green onion
½   teaspoon garlic powder
Salt, to taste
14-16 slices fresh white bread, crusts removed
1   (8-ounce) package cream cheese, room temperature

In a small bowl, mix salmon and mayonnaise. Add celery, onion and garlic powder; mix thoroughly. Add salt, if needed. Add more mayonnaise (or a little sour cream) until a nice consistency is reached (sour cream will add moisture without mayonnaise taste).

Roll each bread slice flat with a rolling pin. Spread some cream cheese, then some salmon mixture on each bread slice. Roll each slice up into a log. Cover and refrigerate. When ready to serve, cut each log into 4 or 5 slices.

Serving suggestion: Place roll-ups on a tray with an assortment of cheese cubes and fruit. Serve with toothpicks to skewer the roll-ups.

Smoked Salmon Pâté

Serves 8

Use the same ingredients as Smoked Salmon Roll-ups (above), except omit cream cheese and bread. Mix all ingredients together and place in a small serving bowl. Serve with a variety of crackers.

Turtleback Farm Inn

T urtleback Farm Inn is a country farmhouse located on Orcas Island, the loveliest of the San Juan Islands which dot the sparkling waters of Puget Sound. This graceful and comfortable inn offers seven bedrooms, each decorated with a blend of fine antiques and contemporary pieces. The inn is considered one of the most romantic places in the country.

As the day ends, guests are offered a glass of sherry, a cheery fire and a game of chess, cards or Scrabble.

INNKEEPERS:	William & Susan C. Fletcher
ADDRESS:	1981 Crow Valley Road
	Eastsound (Orcas Island), WA 98245
TELEPHONE:	(360) 376-4914; (800) 376-4914 (reservations)
E-MAIL:	info@turtlebackinn.com
WEBSITE:	www.turtlebackinn.com
ROOMS:	11 Rooms; All with private baths
CHILDREN:	Children age 8 and older are welcome
ANIMALS:	Not allowed; Resident dog, sheep, cows, chickens
HANDICAPPED:	Is handicapped accessible
DIETARY NEEDS:	Will accommodate guests' special dietary needs

Portobello Purses

Makes 44 Purses

½ stick (¼ cup) butter
1 portobello mushroom, diced
½ cup minced yellow onion
1 tablespoon minced shallot
Salt and pepper, to taste
¼ cup sherry
¼ cup ground walnuts
1 package filo pastry sheets
Melted butter (enough to coat filo sheets)

Preheat oven to 375°F. In a large skillet, melt butter over medium-high heat. Add mushroom, onion and shallot. Season with salt and pepper. Cook until onions are translucent, about 4-5 minutes (watch carefully so the mixture does not burn). Add sherry and ground walnuts; reduce heat and simmer until liquid is almost evaporated. Let cool at room temperature.

On a clean surface, lay 1 filo sheet and brush it with melted butter. Top with a second sheet and brush with butter. Repeat again so you have a stack of 3 buttered sheets. Cut into 2-inch squares. Spoon a little mushroom mixture onto the middle of each square. Grab the 4 corners of a square, pull them together and pinch them closed, forming a purse. Repeat with remaining filo squares. Brush a little butter on the outside of each purse and bake until golden brown, about 10-12 minutes.

Mountain Home Lodge

An array of outdoor activities, first-class dining and friendly service make Mountain Home Lodge a serene resort for all seasons. Spring, summer and fall colors provide stunning backdrops for hiking, mountain biking, whitewater rafting, horseback riding, fishing, swimming and tennis.

Rated one of the region's most romantic getaways, the Lodge is also an ideal setting for small group seminars, weddings and family reunions.

INNKEEPERS:	Brad & Kathy Schmidt
ADDRESS:	8201 Mountain Home Road
	Leavenworth, WA 98826
TELEPHONE:	(509) 548-7077; (800) 414-2378
E-MAIL:	info@mthome.com
WEBSITE:	www.mthome.com
ROOMS:	9 Rooms; 1 Suite; 2 Cabins; All with private baths
CHILDREN:	Call ahead
ANIMALS:	Not allowed
HANDICAPPED:	Not handicapped accessible
DIETARY NEEDS:	Will accommodate guests' special dietary needs

Kathy's Basil Crostini

Makes 30-40 Appetizers

Make one batch of crostini with regular basil pesto and another batch with sun-dried tomato pesto. Some crostini will be green and some will be red – perfect for holiday entertaining. To "dress" them up, put a small sliver of basil and/or sun-dried tomato on top of each crostini after broiling.

¾   **cup mayonnaise**
¼   **cup finely grated Parmesan cheese**
2-5 **tablespoons basil or sun-dried tomato pesto**
French baguette bread, thinly sliced

Preheat broiler. In a small bowl, mix mayonnaise, cheese and pesto together (you can add more cheese or pesto to your taste.) Lightly toast baguette slices on 1 side under broiler. Generously spread pesto mixture on untoasted side of bread and broil for about 3 minutes, or until bubbly. Serve hot.

Optional cooking method: Preheat oven to 400°F. Bake crostini for 10-15 minutes, or until light brown and crisp around edges.

Variation: Finely diced oil-packed sun-dried tomatoes (drained) can be added to regular pesto sauce.

Make-ahead tip: The pesto mixture can be made several days in advance, covered and refrigerated.

Beachside

Beachside Bed and Breakfast is the perfect getaway for a romantic overnight or a special vacation. From the chintz-covered furniture to the flower gardens on the private patio, guests are surrounded by the ambiance of a traditional English cottage.

Amenities include a fully-equipped kitchen, fireplace, large hot tub, an extended continental breakfast and a deep moorage buoy for boaters.

INNKEEPERS:	Doreen & Dick Samuelson
ADDRESS:	679 Kamus Drive
	Fox Island, WA 98333
TELEPHONE:	(253) 549-2524
E-MAIL:	Not available
WEBSITE:	www.beachsidebb.com
ROOMS:	1 Suite; Private bath
CHILDREN:	Call ahead
ANIMALS:	Not allowed
HANDICAPPED:	Call ahead
DIETARY NEEDS:	Will accommodate guests' special dietary needs

Crabby Cheese Muffins

Makes 12 Muffin Halves or 48 Appetizers

1   stick (½ cup) butter or margarine, room temperature (the amount
    may be cut back a little, if desired)
1   (5-ounce) jar Old English cheese
½   teaspoon salt, or less to taste
¼   teaspoon garlic powder
2-3 tablespoons mayonnaise
½   pound fresh or imitation crabmeat (or 1 (6-ounce) can crabmeat)
6   English muffins, cut in half

Preheat oven to 350°F. In a medium bowl, mix together butter, cheese, salt, garlic powder and mayonnaise. Stir in crabmeat. Spread on muffin halves. Leave whole for general eating, or cut into fourths for appetizers (at this point, the muffins may be frozen for later use.) Bake for 20 minutes, or until lightly browned and bubbly. The muffins may also be cooked in the microwave until bubbly, but they won't be crisp.

✿ Carol's Corner

Our friend Terri suggests that when a recipe calls for softened butter or cream cheese and you have forgotten to take it out of the refrigerator ahead of time, fill your mixing bowl with hot water, let it stand for a few minutes, then dump the water out and dry the bowl. The warmth from the bowl will help the butter or cream cheese soften as you are mixing it with the other ingredients.

Chinaberry Hill

Located above the city streets of Tacoma, Chinaberry Hill is a grand Victorian estate surrounded by century-old trees, cascading greenery and captivating views of Puget Sound. This urban inn features an extensive collection of period furniture.

Downtown shops, Antique Row and the waterfront are all within a few blocks of this remarkable garden retreat.

INNKEEPERS:	Cecil & Yarrow Wayman
ADDRESS:	302 Tacoma Avenue North
	North Tacoma, WA 98403
TELEPHONE:	(253) 272-1282
E-MAIL:	chinaberry@wa.net
WEBSITE:	www.chinaberryhill.com
ROOMS:	1 Room; 4 Suites; All with private baths
CHILDREN:	Children welcome in the guest cottage
ANIMALS:	Not allowed; Resident cats
HANDICAPPED:	Not handicapped accessible
DIETARY NEEDS:	Will accommodate guests' special dietary needs

Jalapeño Swirls

Approximately 120 Bite-size Appetizers

"Whenever we serve these, at least 1 or 2 people will come up and demand the recipe. When we share the process with them, it's always met with amazement – that something so simple can have such an elegant appeal. Fair warning: make plenty, people will eat a lot of these – they're irresistible!" ~ Yarrow Wayman, Chinaberry Hill

1   (7-ounce) can chopped green chiles, drained
1   tablespoon diced jalapeño peppers, or to taste (watch out, they'll get hotter after sitting in the cream cheese for awhile)
2   (8-ounce) packages cream cheese, room temperature
1   (10-count) package extra large (burrito size) flour tortillas (the colored wraps are fun!)

Preheat oven to 200°F. In a medium bowl, mix green chiles, jalapeñoes and cream cheese. Wrap tortillas in foil to keep moist and heat briefly in oven until pliable. Spread cream cheese mixture across tortillas, avoiding outer left and right edges, then roll up each tortilla tightly. Place rolled tortillas on a platter, cover with plastic wrap and chill for at least 30 minutes. Slice into ½-inch slices, discarding ends. Lay swirls flat on an appetizer plate, so that the swirl pattern is face up.

Make-ahead tip: To make a day in advance, wrap each individual tortilla roll tightly in plastic wrap and refrigerate.

Carol's Corner
Have fun, be adventurous! The filling combinations for this basic recipe are almost limitless – for a touch of the Pacific Northwest, try a combination of cream cheese, smoked salmon and diced green onions. Another sure-fire winner is diced red pepper, green onions and sliced black olives.

Abendblume Pension

The rooms at the Abendblume Pension Bed and Breakfast are spacious and comfortable. French doors open to a private balcony in the Rosengarten Room. Pine walls and a large river rock fireplace highlight the decor in the Tannenbaum Room.

Breakfast is tastefully prepared and served each morning in the traditional Austrian breakfast room.

INNKEEPERS:	Renee Sexauer
ADDRESS:	12570 Ranger Road
	Leavenworth, WA 98826
TELEPHONE:	(509) 548-4059; (800) 669-7634
EMAIL:	abendblm@rightathome.com
WEBSITE:	www.abendblume.com
ROOMS:	7 Rooms; 4 Suites; All with private baths
CHILDREN:	Not allowed
ANIMALS:	Not allowed
HANDICAPPED:	Not handicapped accessible
DIETARY NEEDS:	Will accommodate guests' special dietary needs

Tomatillo and Tomato Salsa

Makes About 3½ Cups

A tomatillo is often called a Mexican green tomato. It is similar to a small green tomato in size, shape and appearance, but is covered with a thin parchment-like husk. Its flavor could best be described as a combination of apple, lemon and herbs. Tomatillos are available in most supermarkets or specialty produce stores.

1	large clove garlic, minced
2-6	jalapeño peppers (seeds and membranes removed), minced
4	small tomatillos, papery husks removed, washed and diced
6	plum tomatoes, diced (about 2½ cups)
1	medium onion, finely diced (about ½ cup)
½	green bell pepper, finely diced (about ¼ cup)
2	tablespoons coarsely chopped fresh parsley
2	tablespoons coarsely chopped fresh cilantro

Juice of 1 lime (about 2 tablespoons)
½   teaspoon salt, or more to taste

Combine all ingredients in a medium bowl. The salsa can be served immediately, but it will be even better if flavors are allowed to marry by chilling for several hours or overnight in the refrigerator.

Carol's Corner

Wash your hands thoroughly after removing the seeds and membranes from the jalapeño peppers (or wear rubber gloves). Otherwise, the oils from the peppers can cause a burning sensation to your eyes if you touch them. If this should happen, flush your eyes immediately with water.

Caswell's on the Bay

Guests of Caswell's on the Bay Bed and Breakfast relax in the spacious parlor with its breathtaking views of Willapa Bay, Long Island and the Coastal Mountains. This private getaway is a perfect setting for weddings, family reunions and group meetings.

Special features include freshly pressed cotton sheets and the finest Caswell-Massey amenities.

INNKEEPERS:	Bob & Marilyn Caswell
ADDRESS:	25204 Sandridge Road
	Ocean Park, WA 98640
TELEPHONE:	(360) 665-6535; (888) 553-2319
E-MAIL:	bcaswell@willapabay.org
WEBSITE:	www.caswellsinn.com
ROOMS:	5 Rooms; All with private baths
CHILDREN:	Children age 12 and older are welcome
ANIMALS:	Not allowed
HANDICAPPED:	Not handicapped accessible
DIETARY NEEDS:	Will accommodate guests' special dietary needs

Microwave Caramel Corn

Makes 3½ Quarts

A treat sure to be enjoyed by everyone!

14   cups popped popcorn (about 7 tablespoons unpopped kernels)
1   stick (½ cup) butter
1   cup brown sugar
¼   cup light corn syrup
½   teaspoon salt
½   teaspoon baking powder

Lightly coat a piece of waxed paper (about 24 inches long) with nonstick cooking spray; set aside on counter or tabletop. Pop popcorn until you have the proper amount; discard any unpopped kernels. Place the popped popcorn in a large brown paper grocery bag.

In a medium-size, heavy saucepan, melt butter. Add brown sugar, corn syrup and salt (make sure your pan is large enough, as this mixture bubbles up and "grows"). Bring to a boil over medium-high heat, stirring constantly. Boil for 2 minutes without stirring. Stir and then boil for 2 minutes more without stirring. Remove from heat. Add baking powder and stir thoroughly. Pour caramel mixture over popcorn and shake bag to mix.

Put bag of popcorn in microwave on high for 1 minute. Shake bag to mix and put it back in microwave for 1 minute more. Shake and pour popcorn onto waxed paper. Use a spoon to scrape out any remaining caramel corn stuck to the bag. Let caramel corn cool completely. Store in an airtight container.

Carol's Corner

Air-popped popcorn works great for this recipe. You can also use the low-fat microwave popcorn that comes in bags, but reduce the salt in the recipe to ¼ teaspoon. The caramel corn can be frozen in freezer bags for later use, but if anyone knows it's in the freezer, believe me, it won't last long!

Gaslight Inn

Furnished with museum-quality Arts and Crafts period furniture and authentic Northwest Indian artifacts, the Gaslight Inn is located in the heart of Seattle, just a few blocks from restaurants, theaters and fine shops.

A private, in-ground, heated pool with several decks and interesting plant arrangements is found at the back of the inn.

INNKEEPERS:	Steve Bennett & Trevor Logan
ADDRESS:	1727 15th Avenue
	Seattle, WA 98122
TELEPHONE:	(206) 325-3654
E-MAIL:	innkeepr@gaslight-inn.com
WEBSITE:	www.gaslight-inn.com
ROOMS:	8 Rooms; 7 Suites; Private and shared baths
CHILDREN:	Not allowed
ANIMALS:	Not allowed; Resident dog and cat
HANDICAPPED:	Not handicapped accessible
DIETARY NEEDS:	Will accommodate guests' special dietary needs

Buster's Dog Treats

Makes About Small 60 Treats

These treats will keep for about 10 days in a sealed container in the refrigerator, or longer in the freezer. Try using a small bone-shaped cookie cutter (available at many pet stores) for the treats.

2½	cups whole wheat flour
½	cup powdered milk
1	teaspoon salt
1	teaspoon sugar
¼	teaspoon garlic powder
1	egg, beaten
6	tablespoons oil
2	small jars strained beef or chicken baby food
6-10	tablespoons water

Combine all ingredients; mix well. Knead for about 5 minutes (dough should be firm and pull away from bowl). Roll out to about ⅜-inch thick.

Preheat oven to 375°F. Lightly grease a cookie sheet. Cut dough with a bone-shaped cutter or a cookie cutter. Prick top of each treat with a fork. Bake for 30 minutes. Cool, then seal and store in refrigerator or freezer.

Desserts

Desserts

The Manor Farm Inn

The welcome is warm at The Manor Farm Inn. From the gently winding, tree-lined country road to the stately white house with its manicured lawns, this private oasis offers tranquillity and seclusion from the bustle of Puget Sound's cities.

Guests awaken to the aroma of hot-from-the-oven scones, served with homemade raspberry jam. Later, a three-course gourmet breakfast is served in the dining room.

INNKEEPERS:	Janet Plemmons
ADDRESS:	26069 Big Valley Road NE
	Poulsbo, WA 98370
TELEPHONE:	(360) 779-4628
E-MAIL:	information@manorfarminn.com
WEBSITE:	www.manorfarminn.com
ROOMS:	6 Rooms; All with private baths
CHILDREN:	Children age 16 and older are welcome
ANIMALS:	Not allowed
HANDICAPPED:	Not handicapped accessible
DIETARY NEEDS:	Will accommodate guests' special dietary needs

Blackberry-Apple Crumble

Makes 8 servings

Served warm with ice cream – a real winner!

3   Granny Smith apples, peeled and sliced
1   pound fresh blackberries or 1 (16-ounce) bag frozen blackberries
½   cup sugar
1   teaspoon cinnamon

Topping:
1½ cups flour
1½ cups brown sugar
¾   cup rolled oats
1½ sticks (¾ cup) butter, melted

Preheat oven to 350°F. Coat a 13x9-inch baking dish with nonstick cooking spray. Place apples in bottom of dish, then top with blackberries.

In a small bowl, mix sugar and cinnamon; sprinkle over blackberries and apples. In a large bowl, mix together all topping ingredients. Crumble over blackberries and apples. Bake for 60 minutes, or until top is golden brown.

⚘ Carol's Corner
This luscious dessert showcases two of Washington's most delectable fruits – apples and blackberries. The combination of flavors is most pleasing. This recipe doesn't take long to put together and yet it feeds a crowd.

Island Escape

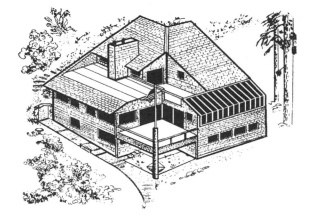

Nestled on the bluffs of Puget Sound, Island Escape Bed and Breakfast features a one-room suite that includes a separate living room with a gas fireplace. This romantic getaway is beautifully landscaped with an array of seasonal flowers.

Guests select a savory breakfast from an assortment of gourmet meals that is served outside their door at a time of their choosing.

INNKEEPERS:	Paula E. Pascoe
ADDRESS:	210 Island Boulevard
	Fox Island, WA 98333
TELEPHONE:	(253) 549-2044; (877) 549-2044
E-MAIL:	paula@island-escape.com
WEBSITE:	www.island-escape.com
ROOMS:	1 Executive Suite; Private bath
CHILDREN:	Welcome
ANIMALS:	Call ahead
HANDICAPPED:	Not handicapped accessible
DIETARY NEEDS:	Will accommodate guests' special dietary needs

Paula's Easy & Decadent Chocolate Trifle

Makes 10 to 12 Servings

"This dessert presents beautifully in a glass bowl, which reveals every delicious layer. People will be asking for seconds!" ~ Paula Pascoe, Island Escape

1	box chocolate cake mix (with pudding in the mix) or your favorite chocolate cake recipe
3	eggs (number depends on which mix or recipe you use)
⅓	cup oil (amount depends on which mix or recipe you use)
1	(16-ounce) can Hershey's chocolate syrup
6	(1.4-ounce) Hershey's SKOR or Heath bars, crushed
1	(16-ounce) tub Cool Whip, thawed in refrigerator
3	maraschino cherries with stems, drained, for garnish

Grease and flour a 13x9-inch pan. Mix and bake cake per box or recipe instructions. Once cooled, break cake into bite-size pieces and layer ⅓ of cake into a large (8-inches in diameter by 5-inches tall) glass trifle bowl. Pour ⅓ of chocolate syrup over cake pieces. Sprinkle about ⅓ of crushed candy bars over syrup (reserve 1 tablespoon of crushed candy bar for garnish). Spoon a layer of Cool Whip over all. Repeat all layers 2 more times, ending with Cool Whip. Sprinkle reserved candy pieces on top of dessert. Add cherries to complete the decoration. Chill for several hours or overnight.

Make-ahead tip: The trifle can be made ahead up to 2 days in advance, covered and refrigerated.

Carol's Corner

This trifle also be made in individual pieces of clear stemware. Place the stemware on doily covered plates. Top each dessert with a bright red maraschino cherry. Very eye-appealing!

Bosch Gärten

The Bosch Gärten Bed and Breakfast was built in 1992 specifically as a bed and breakfast. Guests gaze out the floor-to-ceiling windows at the arbored rose garden and magnificent Cascade Mountains that tower in the southwest.

The Bavarian Village, with its many unique shops and excellent restaurants, is within easy walking distance.

INNKEEPERS:	Georgeanne & Denny Nichols
ADDRESS:	9846 Dye Road
	Leavenworth, WA 98826
TELEPHONE:	(509) 548-6900; (800) 535-0069
E-MAIL:	innkeeper@boschgarten.com
WEBSITE:	www.boschgarten.com.com
ROOMS:	3 Rooms; All with private baths
CHILDREN:	Call ahead
ANIMALS:	Not allowed
HANDICAPPED:	Not handicapped accessible
DIETARY NEEDS:	Will accommodate guests' special dietary needs

Chocolate Mousse

Makes 8 Servings

This dessert, perfect for chocoholics, is easy to make, but plan ahead as all of the ingredients, as well as the bowl and beaters, must be thoroughly chilled.

⅔ cup chocolate syrup
1¼ cups sweetened condensed milk
2 cups heavy whipping cream
½ teaspoon vanilla
½ cup slivered almonds, for garnish (optional)
Whipped cream, for garnish (optional)
Chocolate shavings, for garnish (optional)

In a large bowl, mix together chocolate syrup, sweetened condensed milk, whipping cream and vanilla. Place in refrigerator, along with beaters, and chill well.

When well chilled, beat mixture until it is thickened and stands in peaks. Spoon mixture into pretty demitasse cups; put in freezer to freeze. Remove from freezer 15-20 minutes before serving. Garnish with a sprinkling of almonds or a dollop of whipped cream and chocolate shavings, if desired.

Fotheringham House

F otheringham House is a late Queen Anne-style house and is a Primary
Site in the Browne's Addition National Historic District. There are tin
ceilings in many rooms and hard and softwood floors. The gardens have
been extensively reworked and now feature Victorian era cutting flowers,
hostas, ferns, fountains, a bird sanctuary and seating.

At one time, the house contained an Otis elevator which ran between the
first and second floors.

INNKEEPERS:	Poul & Irene Jensen
ADDRESS:	2128 West Second Avenue
	Spokane, WA 99204
TELEPHONE:	(509) 838-1891
E-MAIL:	innkeeper@fotheringham.net
WEBSITE:	www.fotheringham.net
ROOMS:	3 Rooms; Private and shared baths
CHILDREN:	Children age 12 and older are welcome
ANIMALS:	Not allowed
HANDICAPPED:	Not handicapped accessible
DIETARY NEEDS:	Will accommodate guests' special dietary needs

Fotheringham House Truffles

Makes 50 to 75 Truffles

It does take practice to make truffles; but it is a fun and delicious practice. Problems with truffles usually arise when the chocolate is too warm. Return to refrigerator when needed. Making truffles in the summer is difficult – you may only be able to coat 15 or 20 before returning the tray to the refrigerator.

1   pound dark or semisweet chocolate, chopped
1   cup whipping cream
2   tablespoons unsalted butter, cut into small pieces
2   tablespoons honey, warmed
2   tablespoons liqueur, such as Kahlúa, Grand Marnier or framboise
8   ounces dipping chocolate (preferable couverture or chocolate appels, available at chocolate shops and some specialty groceries)

Place chocolate in a large bowl. Bring whipping cream just to a boil. Pour over chocolate, stirring constantly (and very slowly) until smooth. Add unsalted butter; stir until melted and smooth.

Mix honey and liqueur; stir into chocolate. Pour into 13x9-inch glass baking dish. Refrigerate until firm, at least 3 hours or preferably overnight.

Cover a sheet pan with parchment paper (available at candy making supply shops). Using a teaspoon, form chocolate into balls by rolling in hands or using a melon baller (keep hands dry and cold by rinsing in cold water, then drying them). Place chocolate balls on parchment paper. Place trays of chocolate balls in refrigerator to chill again (for at least several hours).

Melt half the dipping chocolate in a small, stainless steel bowl placed in a small pan of water over very low heat. Stir chocolate until melted and smooth. Using a cocktail fork, dip chilled truffle balls in chocolate. Twirl over pot so excess coating drips offs. Add more dipping chocolate to pot as needed, returning chocolate balls to refrigerator to keep chilled while coating melts. Arrange coated truffles on a rack lined with clean parchment paper. Refrigerate until set, place in candy paper cups and store in refrigerator.

Turtleback Farm Inn

B reakfast at the Turtleback Farm Inn is served in the farmhouse dining room or on the expansive deck overlooking the valley below and welcoming the morning sun. Tables are set with fine bone china, silver and crisp linen.

The inn can provide lunch and dinner for private parties. The innkeepers are delighted to suggest menus or to recreate a special dinner for a celebration.

INNKEEPERS:	William & Susan C. Fletcher
ADDRESS:	1981 Crow Valley Road
	Eastsound (Orcas Island), WA 98245
TELEPHONE:	(360) 376-4914; (800) 376-4914 (reservations)
E-MAIL:	info@turtlebackinn.com
WEBSITE:	www.turtlebackinn.com
ROOMS:	11 Rooms; All with private baths
CHILDREN:	Children age 8 and older are welcome
ANIMALS:	Not allowed; Resident dog, sheep, cows, chickens
HANDICAPPED:	Is handicapped accessible
DIETARY NEEDS:	Will accommodate guests' special dietary needs

Brownie Pie

Makes 6 to 8 Servings

Often many of us find ourselves with last minute family or friends for dinner. The following recipe provides a quick, rich and tasty solution for dessert.

2	eggs
1	cup sugar
1	stick (½ cup) butter, room temperature
½	cup flour

Pinch of salt

4	tablespoons unsweetened cocoa powder
½	teaspoon instant coffee granules
1	teaspoon vanilla
½	cup chopped walnuts

Vanilla or coffee ice cream (optional)
Whipped cream (optional)

Preheat oven to 325°F. Grease and flour an 8-inch pie pan. Put all ingredients, except walnuts, in food processor. Blend for 2 minutes, scraping down bowl a couple of times. Add walnuts and pulse a couple of times to incorporate.

Pour into pie pan and bake for 30 minutes, or until done. The pie will settle while cooling. When completely cool, cut into wedges and serve with either vanilla or coffee ice cream or whipped cream, if desired.

Willcox House

WILLCOX HOUSE

Built in 1937 by Colonel Julian and Constance Willcox, the Willcox House Country Inn has been restored to its art deco grandeur. Once described as the grand entertainment capital of the canal region, this elegant getaway continues that tradition.

Dinner is available to inn guests and a limited number of visitors. The elaborate four-course chef's choice meals attract diners from around the peninsula.

INNKEEPERS:	Phillip & Cecilia Hughes
ADDRESS:	2390 Tekiu Road NW
	Seabeck, WA 98380
TELEPHONE:	(360) 830-4492; (800) 725-9477
E-MAIL:	Not available
WEBSITE:	www.willcoxhouse.com
ROOMS:	5 Rooms; All with private baths
CHILDREN:	Children age 15 and older are welcome
ANIMALS:	Not allowed
HANDICAPPED:	Not handicapped accessible
DIETARY NEEDS:	Will accommodate guests' special dietary needs

Lemon Pudding Cake

Makes 4 Servings

This refreshing dessert forms two layers as it bakes.

3   eggs
½   stick (¼ cup) butter, melted
1   cup sugar, divided
⅓   cup flour
⅓   cup lemon juice
Grated zest of 1 lemon
1   cup milk, warmed
Raspberries (or other berries of choice)
Whipped cream (optional)
Mint leaves (optional)

Preheat oven to 350°F. Separate eggs, putting egg whites in a small bowl and egg yolks in a large bowl. Beat egg yolks with melted butter and ½ cup of sugar. Alternately add flour and lemon juice. Mix in grated lemon zest; set aside.

Beat egg whites until foamy. Add ½ cup of sugar and beat until glossy and stiff; set aside. Add warmed milk to egg yolk mixture. Then fold egg whites into egg yolk mixture.

Lightly butter or grease a 2-3 quart round, oven-proof bowl or casserole dish. Pour in batter. Set bowl into a pan of hot water and bake for 45 minutes, or until top is lightly browned. Spoon into individual serving dishes and garnish with raspberries. Add a touch of whipped cream and a fresh mint leaf, if desired.

Willcox House

WILLCOX HOUSE

Providing warm hospitality since 1989, the Willcox House is a premier country house inn located between Seattle and the Olympic Peninsula on the Kitsap Peninsula. Surrounded by a natural paradise, every room has a commanding view of the Hood Canal and the Olympic Mountains. The private pier can accommodate boats or float planes.

Activities include combing the oyster-laden beach, swimming and boating.

INNKEEPERS:	Phillip & Cecilia Hughes
ADDRESS:	2390 Tekiu Road NW
	Seabeck, WA 98380
TELEPHONE:	(360) 830-4492; (800) 725-9477
E-MAIL:	Not available
WEBSITE:	www.willcoxhouse.com
ROOMS:	5 Rooms; All with private baths
CHILDREN:	Children age 15 and older are welcome
ANIMALS:	Not allowed
HANDICAPPED:	Not handicapped accessible
DIETARY NEEDS:	Will accommodate guests' special dietary needs

Chocolate Truffle Cake

Makes 10 to 12 Servings

8	ounces semi-sweet baking chocolate
1½	sticks (¾ cup) butter
8	egg whites
6	egg yolks
1	teaspoon vanilla
¼	cup strong brewed coffee, room temperature
2	tablespoons cognac or orange liqueur
⅓	cup flour
¼	teaspoon cream of tartar
¾	cup sugar

Preheat oven to 350°F. In a small, microwaveable bowl, melt chocolate and butter together in microwave on low power, stirring frequently (this step can also be done in a small saucepan over low heat); set aside.

Put egg whites in a large bowl and put egg yolks in another large bowl. Beat egg yolks with vanilla until light in color, about 5 minutes. Mix in coffee. Add cognac alternately with flour. Mix chocolate/butter mixture into egg yolk mixture; set aside.

Beat egg whites with cream of tartar until foamy. Add sugar; beat until egg whites are glossy and form soft peaks. Using a wire whisk, fold a big scoop of egg whites into chocolate mixture. Then gently fold in rest of egg whites.

Grease a 9-inch springform pan. Pour in batter and bake for 60 minutes. Cool completely on wire rack (cake will fall a bit in the middle while cooling). Run a knife around edge of pan and remove outer rim. Cover and refrigerate cake. When ready to serve, bring to room temperature. Serve with fresh berries, berry coulis (purée or sauce) and caramel or vanilla sauce.

Make-ahead tip: Freeze cake on cookie sheet for an hour or so. Then wrap well and freeze for later use. Thaw in refrigerator.

The Highland Inn

Nestled on a wooded hillside, the Highland Inn is a quiet, secluded bed and breakfast located on San Juan Island. This island getaway is home to three resident pods of orca whales. From April through October, the water below the inn is their feeding and playground area.

Whale Watch Park and the Lime Kiln Lighthouse are just a mile up the coast with many hiking trails and picnic spots located along the way.

INNKEEPERS:	Helen King
ADDRESS:	PO Box 135
	Friday Harbor, WA 98250
TELEPHONE:	(360) 378-9450; (888) 400-9850
E-MAIL:	helen@highlandinn.com
WEBSITE:	www.highlandinn.com
ROOMS:	2 Suites; Both with private baths
CHILDREN:	Not allowed
ANIMALS:	Not allowed
HANDICAPPED:	Not handicapped accessible
DIETARY NEEDS:	Will accommodate guests' special dietary needs

Banana Nut Cake

Makes 4 Servings

This deliciously moist cake won Helen King the title of Mrs. Pacific Palisades and later that of Mrs. Bay Area in the Mrs. America Baking competition. In the final competition, she was first runner-up for the State of California.

3	cups sifted cake flour
½	teaspoon baking powder
¾	teaspoon baking soda
1¼	teaspoons salt
1	cup shortening
2	cups sugar
2	eggs, slightly beaten
¾	cup buttermilk
1½	cups mashed banana
¾	cup toasted chopped walnuts (save ¼ cup for topping)

Cream cheese frosting (recipe follows)

Preheat oven to 350°F. Sift together cake flour, baking powder, baking soda and salt on a piece of waxed paper. Cream together shortening, sugar and eggs; beat until light and fluffy. Add buttermilk alternately with sifted dry ingredients. Cream mashed banana until almost liquid and smooth; fold into batter along with nuts. Pour into 3 greased and floured 9-inch cake pans. Bake for 25 to 30 minutes, or until cake springs back to the touch. Cool cakes. When cakes are cooled, brush off crumbs and frost and layer cakes. Then frost sides and top and decorate with toasted walnuts.

Cream cheese frosting:

½	stick (¼ cup) butter, room temperature
3	ounces cream cheese, room temperature
2	cups sifted powdered sugar

Pinch of salt

½	teaspoon vanilla

In a large bowl, beat together butter and cream cheese. Slowly add powdered sugar and salt, continuing to beat well. Mix in vanilla.

MacKaye Harbor Inn

Tranquillity, romance and a touch of nostalgia await the guests of the MacKaye Harbor Inn. Built in 1904 and completely restored in 1985, this charming inn offers five beautifully decorated guest rooms, each reminiscent of the inn's past.

The carriage house, built in 1991, has added two large luxury accommodations in the same MacKaye Harbor Inn tradition.

INNKEEPERS:	Robin & Mike Bergstrom
ADDRESS:	949 MacKaye, PO Box 1940
	Lopez Island, WA 98261
TELEPHONE:	(360) 468-2253; (888) 314-6140
E-MAIL:	innkeeper@mackayeharborinn.com
WEBSITE:	www.mackayeharborinn.com
ROOMS:	4 Rooms; 1 Suite; 2 Cottages; Private and shared baths
CHILDREN:	Children age 9 and older are welcome
ANIMALS:	Not allowed
HANDICAPPED:	Not handicapped accessible
DIETARY NEEDS:	Will accommodate guests' special dietary needs

Cowboy Cookies

Makes 48 (3-inch) Cookies

"I can make these with my eyes shut! This cookie has become the standby for the inn. People never turn down a chocolate chip cookie, especially one fresh from the oven, and with healthy oatmeal in it." ~ Robin Bergstrom, MacKaye Harbor Inn

1	cup sugar
1	cup brown sugar
1	cup shortening
3	eggs
1	teaspoon vanilla
2	cups flour
½	teaspoon baking powder
1	teaspoon baking soda
½	teaspoon salt
2	cups rolled oats
2	cups chocolate chips

Preheat oven to 350°F. In a large bowl, beat together sugar, brown sugar and shortening. Mix in eggs and vanilla. Sift in flour, baking powder, baking soda and salt. Add oats and mix well. Stir in chocolate chips.

Drop dough onto greased cookie sheet and bake for approximately 15 minutes. Let rest on cookie sheet for a couple minutes and then transfer cookies to a wire rack to cool.

> *Carol's Corner*
> *Try dropping the dough onto the cookie sheet with a small ice cream scoop (1¾-inches in diameter) – it's easy and makes uniform-size cookies.*

Spring Bay Inn

E arly risers at the Spring Bay Inn on Orcas Island are treated to a breakfast that includes homemade pastries, fresh fruits, coffee and tea. Brunch, also included, is served family-style in the bay-front dining room.

Weather permitting, a daily kayak tour provides guests a unique way to explore the natural beauty of the island's waterfront.

INNKEEPERS:	Carl Burger & Sandy Playa
ADDRESS:	464 Spring Bay Trail
	Olga, Orcas Island WA 98279
TELEPHONE:	(360) 376-5531
E-MAIL:	info@springbayinn.com
WEBSITE:	www.springbayinn.com
ROOMS:	5 Rooms; All with private baths
CHILDREN:	Welcome (Must be over age 10 to kayak)
ANIMALS:	Not allowed
HANDICAPPED:	Not handicapped accessible
DIETARY NEEDS:	Will accommodate guests' special dietary needs

Oatmeal Raisin Cookies

Makes About 36 (3-inch) Cookies

For variety, try dried cranberries or craisins in place of the raisins.

1	cup (2 sticks) butter, melted
2	cups brown sugar
2	eggs
2	teaspoons vanilla
1½	cups flour
1	teaspoon salt
1	teaspoon baking soda
1	teaspoon cinnamon
3	cups rolled oats
1	cup walnuts
1	cup raisins

Preheat oven to 375°F. In a large bowl, mix together melted butter, brown sugar, eggs and vanilla. Sift in flour, salt, soda and cinnamon; mix well. Stir in oats, nuts and raisins.

Drop dough by spoonfuls onto a greased cookie sheet and bake for about 10 minutes. (Note: Take cookies out of oven just before they look fully cooked – they will firm up as they cool.) Leave cookies on cookie sheet for several minutes to cool before removing to wire rack.

Duffy House

The Duffy House Bed and Breakfast is a 1920s Tudor-style home that is conveniently located on a scenic jogging and bicycling loop that begins and ends at the ferry terminal. A full breakfast, featuring fresh baked goods, complements the inn experience.

Local activities include golfing, sportfishing, sailing, whale watching from strategic settings, exploring tidal pools, following the flight of a bald eagle or biking the byways.

INNKEEPERS:	Arthur Miller
ADDRESS:	4214 Pear Point Road
	Friday Harbor, WA
TELEPHONE:	(360) 378-5604; (800) 972-2089
E-MAIL:	duffyhouse@rockisland.com
WEBSITE:	www.duffyhouse.com
ROOMS:	5 Rooms; All with private baths
CHILDREN:	Call ahead
ANIMALS:	Not allowed
HANDICAPPED:	Not handicapped accessible
DIETARY NEEDS:	Will accommodate guests' special dietary needs

Snickerdoodles

Makes About 48 (3½-inch) Cookies

These cookies are crisp around the edges, yet remain soft and chewy in the middle. Bet you can't eat just one!

2	sticks (1 cup) butter, room temperature
2	cups sugar
2	eggs
3	cups flour
2	teaspoons cream of tartar
1	teaspoon baking soda

Topping:

¼	cup sugar
2	teaspoons cinnamon

Preheat oven to 400°F. In a large bowl, beat together butter and sugar. Add eggs, one at a time, beating well after each addition. Sift in flour, cream of tartar and baking soda. Mix well, then chill.

Drop dough 2-inches apart (the cookies spread while baking) on an ungreased cookie sheet. Press flat using fingertips or heel of hand.

Combine topping ingredients; sprinkle on top of cookies. Bake for 6-7 minutes (they will be pale and not look done). Let rest on the cookie sheet for 1-2 minutes, then remove to a wire rack to cool.

> *Carol's Corner*
> *Ten-year-old neighbor Charlee dropped by one day while I was testing this recipe. Valuing her opinion, I gave her some Snickerdoodles and asked her to let me know what she thought. After she and her family tasted them, she reported, "This recipe should be in the book!" So, Charlee, here it is. This one's especially for you!*

MacKaye Harbor Inn

The MacKaye Harbor Inn is a quiet retreat for those seeking comfort, beauty and peace. Located on Lopez Island, this private getaway has been a beacon showing safe harbor to sailors, fishermen and travelers since the turn-of-the-century.

Special comforts include a water view from the spacious parlor, down comforters, a beverage bar, guest refrigerator and a bountiful breakfast.

INNKEEPERS:	Robin & Mike Bergstrom
ADDRESS:	949 MacKaye, PO Box 1940
	Lopez Island, WA 98261
TELEPHONE:	(360) 468-2253; (888) 314-6140
E-MAIL:	innkeeper@mackayeharborinn.com
WEBSITE:	www.mackayeharborinn.com
ROOMS:	4 Rooms; 1 Suite; 2 Cottages; Private and shared baths
CHILDREN:	Children age 9 and older are welcome
ANIMALS:	Not allowed
HANDICAPPED:	Not handicapped accessible
DIETARY NEEDS:	Will accommodate guests' special dietary needs

Coconut Shortbread

Makes About 24 Wedge-Shaped Cookies

Buttery and rich — perfect with afternoon tea!

4   cups sweetened coconut
2   cups flour
½   cup plus 1 tablespoon sugar
1   teaspoon salt
2   sticks (1 cup) unsalted butter, room temperature
1½   teaspoons vanilla

Lightly butter two 9-inch tart pans with removable bottoms. In a large bowl, mix coconut, flour, sugar and salt. Add butter and vanilla; beat well with an electric mixer. Divide dough between pans and press to cover bottoms. Refrigerate for 15 minutes.

Preheat oven to 350°F. Bake shortbread for 30-40 minutes. Remove pan sides and cut shortbread into wedges. If wedges are moist, place on cookie sheet and bake until crisp, about 7 minutes more. Store shortbread in an airtight container at room temperature.

Gaslight Inn

GASLIGHT INN

In restoring Gaslight Inn, the innkeepers brought out the home's original turn-of-the-century ambiance and warmth, while keeping in mind the additional conveniences and contemporary style needed by today's travelers. The interior is appointed in exacting detail, with strikingly rich, dark colors, oak paneling and an enormous entryway and staircase.

"Few bed and breakfast inns anywhere equal the elegance and amenities of the Gaslight Inn." ~ The Bed and Breakfast Traveler

INNKEEPERS:	Steve Bennett & Trevor Logan
ADDRESS:	1727 15th Avenue
	Seattle, WA 98122
TELEPHONE:	(206) 325-3654
E-MAIL:	innkeepr@gaslight-inn.com
WEBSITE:	www.gaslight-inn.com
ROOMS:	8 Rooms; 7 Suites; Private and shared baths
CHILDREN:	Not allowed
ANIMALS:	Not allowed; Resident dog and cat
HANDICAPPED:	Not handicapped accessible
DIETARY NEEDS:	Will accommodate guests' special dietary needs

Almond Shortbread Cookies

Makes 36 to 48 Cookies

These are delicious and easy, especially if you use a mixer. We love the flavor and texture that the nuts give the cookies – it's lighter than regular shortbread.

1½ cups all-purpose flour
2 sticks (1 cup) butter, room temperature
¼ teaspoon salt
½ cup sugar
1 cup ground almonds (about ¼ pound almonds with skin-on)
Powdered sugar for dusting

Preheat oven to 350°F. Combine flour, butter, salt and sugar; mix with a fork or a mixer with a paddle attachment. Add ground almonds and mix together. Knead into a firm dough. Form into approximately 1¼-inch balls. Place on cookie sheet and flatten to approximately ¼-inch thick with a fork or the bottom of a glass. Bake for 10-14 minutes. Cool on rack. Dust with powdered sugar while still warm.

The Inn at Burg's Landing

The logo for The Inn at Burg's Landing consists of a silhouette of two majestic evergreens that were planted in 1929 by Chester and Edna Burg in celebration of their wedding day. These trees represent the inn's steadfast commitment to the Burg family's heritage of warm, friendly and personal hospitality toward all guests who share this island refuge.

Guests enjoy spectacular views of Mount Rainier, the Cascades and Puget Sound.

INNKEEPERS:	Ken & Annie Burg
ADDRESS:	8808 Villa Beach Road
	Anderson Island, WA 98303
TELEPHONE:	(253) 884-9185; (800) 431-5622
E-MAIL:	innatburgslanding@mailexcite.com
WEBSITE:	www.burgslandingbb.com
ROOMS:	4 Rooms; Private and shared baths
CHILDREN:	Welcome
ANIMALS:	Not allowed
HANDICAPPED:	Not handicapped accessible
DIETARY NEEDS:	Will accommodate guests' special dietary needs

Biscotti

Makes About 40 Biscotti

Vary the taste of these twice-baked crunchy Italian cookies by using different extract flavorings. Great for dipping in coffee!

4	cups flour
1	cup sugar
1½	teaspoons baking powder
¼	teaspoon salt
4	eggs
1	cup oil
3	teaspoons vanilla (or almond, orange or anise flavorings)
¼	cup coarsely chopped almonds

Semi-sweet chocolate (optional)
Crushed almonds (optional)

Preheat oven 375°F. In a large bowl, sift together flour, sugar, baking powder and salt. In a small bowl, lightly beat together eggs, oil and vanilla. Add egg mixture and chopped almonds to dry ingredients. Stir until combined.

Divide dough into 4 equal pieces. Form into loaves, each about 3-inches wide and 1½-inches high. Place 3 or 4 inches apart on an ungreased cookie sheet. Bake for 20-25 minutes.

Remove from oven and let cool for 10 minutes. Transfer loaves to cutting board. With serrated knife, cut each loaf crosswise into ½-inch thick diagonal slices. Place slices cut-side down on cookie sheet in a single layer and bake for an additional 10-15 minutes, or until golden brown, turning once. Transfer to wire racks; cool completely. Store in an airtight container.

For chocolate-dipped biscotti: Melt semi-sweet chocolate in a microwave oven or in a double boiler over low heat on the stovetop. Dip tops, sides or bottoms of biscotti into chocolate. If desired, sprinkle some crushed almonds over chocolate. Refrigerate biscotti about 30 minutes to set chocolate. Store in a tightly covered container.

Trumpeter Inn

Named for the magnificent trumpeter swans that grace the nearby marshlands during the winter, the Trumpeter Inn Bed and Breakfast features panoramic views of False Bay and the snow-capped Olympic Mountains. Located within a mile of Friday Harbor, this lovely inn is a designated Backyard Wild Bird Sanctuary.

Amenities include plush bathrobes, fresh flowers, chocolate truffles and down comforters. A wheelchair accessible suite is also available.

INNKEEPERS:	Mark Zipkin & Aylene Geringer
ADDRESS:	318 Trumpeter Way
	Friday Harbor, WA 98250
TELEPHONE:	(800) 826-7926
E-MAIL:	swan@rockisland.com
WEBSITE:	www.trumpeterinn.com
ROOMS:	6 Rooms; All with private baths
CHILDREN:	Children age 12 and older are welcome
ANIMALS:	Not allowed
HANDICAPPED:	Is handicapped accessible
DIETARY NEEDS:	Will accommodate guests' special dietary needs

Almond Roca Cookies

Makes 36 (2-inch) Cookies

These cookies taste exactly like Almond Roca candy! And it's a good thing they are so easy to make, because everyone in your family will be clamoring for them. All you do is mix up the dough, press it in a baking pan and bake it. The chocolate chips you sprinkle on the baked dough just when it comes out of the oven melt to make a delicious chocolate icing. A sprinkling of almonds completes this tasty cookie.

2	sticks (1 cup) butter, room temperature
½	cup brown sugar
½	cup white sugar
1	teaspoon vanilla
1	egg yolk
1	cup flour
1	teaspoon baking powder
12	ounces chocolate chips
¼	cup chopped almonds

Preheat oven to 325°F. Lightly grease a 13x10-inch rimmed cookie sheet or jelly roll pan. Cream together butter and brown and white sugars. Add vanilla and egg yolk; blend thoroughly. Mix flour, baking powder and salt together, then stir it into the butter mixture. When completely mixed, press dough into prepared baking dish.

Bake until dough begins to brown, about 25 minutes. Remove from oven and sprinkle chocolate chips over entire surface. Spread chocolate evenly as it melts. Sprinkle with almonds and return pan to the oven for a few minutes. Cool cookies in the pan until chocolate is firm (on hot days, you may have to put the pan in the refrigerator to cool). Cut into 2-inch squares to serve.

The Highland Inn

The Highland Inn has a very private setting which is the perfect location to celebrate an anniversary, honeymoon or just a quiet getaway surrounded by the beauty of the Pacific Northwest. A gourmet breakfast is served each morning in your suite, in the dining room or on the covered veranda overlooking the sea.

Afternoon tea and fresh baked cookies welcome you on arrival or when you return from an exciting day of exploring the island.

INNKEEPERS:	Helen King
ADDRESS:	PO Box 135
	Friday Harbor, WA 98250
TELEPHONE:	(360) 378-9450; (888) 400-9850
E-MAIL:	helen@highlandinn.com
WEBSITE:	www.highlandinn.com
ROOMS:	2 Suites; Both with private baths
CHILDREN:	Not allowed
ANIMALS:	Not allowed
HANDICAPPED:	Not handicapped accessible
DIETARY NEEDS:	Will accommodate guests' special dietary needs

Mrs. King's Cookies

Makes About 60 Cookies

"These cookies were featured in the November 1990 issue of Family Circle Magazine *and in Rose Levy Beranbaum's* Rose's Christmas Cookies. *In the last year that I had the Babbling Brook Inn in Santa Cruz, California, over 9,000 cookies were baked for guests. They are still served each day here at the Highland Inn of San Juan Island. The dough will keep refrigerated or frozen — bake them fresh as needed." ~ Helen King, Highland Inn*

2	sticks (1 cup) butter
1	cup brown sugar
1	cup white sugar
2	eggs
1	teaspoon vanilla

Grated zest and juice of ½ orange

2	cups flour
1	teaspoon baking powder
1	teaspoon salt
1	teaspoon baking soda
1	cup white chocolate chips
1	cup semi-sweet chocolate chips
1½	cups raisins
1½	cups chopped nuts
1	cup old-fashioned rolled oats
1½	cups orange almond granola, or any good granola

Preheat oven to 350°F. Blend butter and brown and white sugars until creamy. Add eggs, vanilla and orange juice and zest; beat until well mixed.

Sift together flour, baking powder, salt and baking soda. Stir into the egg and butter mixture. Mix until just blended. Add white and semi-sweet chocolate chips, raisins, nuts, oats and granola; mix well.

Shape into ping pong or golf ball size balls and bake on an ungreased cookie sheet for 8-10 minutes, or until just turning brown around the edges. These cookies are best served warm from the oven.

Guest House Log Cottages

Located on 25 acres of forest and meadow with marine and mountain views, the Guest House Log Cottages are enchanting romantic getaways. Each cottage is uniquely designed for one couple in a private setting and includes a fireplace, kitchen and Jacuzzi. An outdoor swimming pool, hot tub and small exercise room are also provided.

"We feel like we just spent time in a fairy tale." ~ Guest, Guest House Log Cottages

INNKEEPERS:	Peggy Walker & Karen Holdsworth
ADDRESS:	24371 SR 525
	Greenbank, Whidbey Island, WA 98253
TELEPHONE:	(360) 678-3115
E-MAIL:	guesthse@whidbey.net
WEBSITE:	www.guesthouselogcottages.com
ROOMS:	6 Cottages; All with private baths
CHILDREN:	Not allowed
ANIMALS:	Not allowed
HANDICAPPED:	Not handicapped accessible
DIETARY NEEDS:	Will accommodate guests' special dietary needs

Jam Kolaches

Makes 24 Kolaches

These are quick and easy, and are great for breakfast or tea.

1   stick (½ cup) butter
1   3-ounce package cream cheese, room temperature
1¼   cups flour
Jam, your favorite
Powdered sugar

Preheat oven to 375°F. Cream together butter and cream cheese until light and fluffy. Mix in flour. Roll out dough to ¼-inch thick. Cut into 2-inch rounds with a cookie cutter or glass.

Place rounds on a greased cookie sheet. Spoon ½-1 teaspoon jam onto each round. Fold the 2 sides of the rounds over, overlapping slightly. Bake for 15 minutes. Remove from oven and sprinkle with powdered sugar.

Old Favorites from the First Edition

Old Favorites from the First Edition

Peaches Supreme

Makes 3 to 6 servings

Peach topping:
½   cup brown sugar
½   cup chopped pecans
1   stick (½ cup) butter, melted
½   cup rolled oats
½   cup granola (with dates and raisins)

Peaches:
1   (20-ounce) can peach halves, drained (usually 6 halves)
6   teaspoons brown sugar, divided
1   (6-ounce) container custard-style vanilla yogurt
6   tablespoons raspberry jam (homemade jam is best)

To prepare peach topping: Preheat broiler. Combine, in a small bowl, brown sugar, pecans, butter, oats and granola. Mix well and set aside.

To make peaches: Arrange peach halves, round-sides-down, in a shallow baking dish or a pie pan. Place 1 teaspoon brown sugar in each peach. Broil for 2-3 minutes – watch carefully! Remove from broiler.

Top each peach half with a heaping spoonful of peach topping. Broil for 1-3 minutes more, until topping begins to turn brown – watch carefully! Remove from broiler and top each peach half with 1 tablespoon vanilla yogurt and 1 tablespoon jam.

Serving suggestion: Attractively arrange each peach half on a bed of green leafy lettuce. Very colorful!

Potato Pancakes

Makes 2 servings

Ingredients can be easily doubled or tripled.

2	medium potatoes, grated
2	tablespoons finely chopped onion
2	teaspoons flour
½	teaspoon baking powder
2	eggs, lightly beaten
2	teaspoons sour cream
2	tablespoons chopped pecans
2	tablespoons vegetable oil

In a medium bowl, combine potato and onion. Mix in flour and baking powder. Add eggs, sour cream and pecans; mix thoroughly.

Heat 1 tablespoon of oil in skillet over medium to medium-high heat. Place enough batter in pan to make 4 thin pancakes. Cook until bottoms of pancakes are very crisp, about 5-6 minutes. Turn and cook other side until crisp. Repeat with other half of oil and batter.

Serving suggestions: Potato pancakes are great with butter, maple syrup, applesauce and sausage or bacon.

Polish Apple Pancakes with Marionberry Butter

Makes 4 Servings (About 10 Pancakes)

1	cup flour
1	tablespoon sugar
½	teaspoon salt
1	egg
1	cup milk
1	tablespoon oil
3	tablespoons butter
5	medium apples, peeled and thinly sliced
¼	cup brown sugar

Marionberry butter (recipe follows)
Powdered sugar
Maple syrup

In a food processor, combine flour, sugar, salt, egg, milk and oil. Blend until smooth, about 1 minute. Pour batter into a large bowl; set aside. In a heavy skillet, melt butter. Add apples, sprinkle with brown sugar and cook for about 2 minutes, or until slightly cooked. Strain excess liquid. Add apples to batter; stir until apples are completely coated. (If you are not making pancakes right away, cover batter with plastic wrap so apples do not turn brown.)

On a hot, lightly greased skillet, pour batter by ¼-cupfuls and spread to form 5-inch circles. When surface of pancake is no longer shiny, turn and cook other side until apples are semi-soft and pancakes are golden brown. Serve with marionberry butter, a dusting of powdered sugar and maple syrup.

Marionberry butter:

1	stick (1/2 cup) butter, room temperature
¼	cup marionberry jam (or other favorite "no seed" jam or preserves)

In food processor, whip butter until smooth. Add jam to taste and whip until blended.

Patti's Porridge

Makes 6 to 8 Servings

The topping for this oatmeal will convert the most skeptical of oatmeal eaters!
Serve with a pitcher of milk for those who like it.

Quick-cooking oatmeal (enough for 6-8 people)
Water
Salt
½   stick (¼ cup) margarine
¾   cup brown sugar
1   tablespoon cinnamon, or less to taste
2-3   bananas, sliced

Prepare oatmeal for 6-8 people according to package directions.

To make banana sauce: In a medium skillet, melt margarine; stir in brown sugar and cinnamon until combined. Stir just until mixture starts bubbling around edges, then remove from heat and stir in bananas.

Put oatmeal in a large serving bowl (or individual bowls) and pour banana sauce over top of oatmeal.

Peppercorn-Crusted Salmon with White Wine Butter Sauce

Makes 4 Servings

1½   cups water
1   cup light or dark brown sugar
3   tablespoons coarse salt, such as sea or kosher
1   tablespoon Liquid Smoke
1   tablespoon grated fresh ginger
3   bay leaves
1   teaspoon whole allspice
4   salmon fillets (about 2 pounds)
3   tablespoons cracked black peppercorns
2   tablespoons plus 2 teaspoons honey
White wine butter sauce (recipe follows)
4   sprigs fresh dill, for garnish (optional)

In medium saucepan, combine water, brown sugar, salt, Liquid Smoke, ginger, bay leaves and allspice. Bring to boil, reduce heat and simmer until sugar is dissolved, about 5 minutes. Remove from heat and cool for at least 15 minutes.

Place salmon in a glass baking dish. Pour marinade over salmon; cover and refrigerate for 6 hours, or overnight, turning salmon occasionally. Line a baking sheet with parchment paper. Remove salmon from marinade, reserving marinade. Pat salmon fillets dry with paper towels. Place fillets skin-side-down on baking sheet. Strain reserved marinade into a saucepan; discard solids. Add peppercorns. Bring to a boil. Reduce heat and simmer for 10 minutes. Strain, reserving peppercorns; discard liquid. Spread honey over tops of salmon; sprinkle with reserved peppercorns.

Preheat oven to 350°F. While oven is preheating, start making white wine butter sauce. (It will take 25 minutes – don't try to skimp on cooking time or the sauce will not be thick enough.) Bake salmon for 20-25 minutes, or until fish flakes easily.

Recipe continues on page 299…

To serve: On each plate, pour a circle of white wine butter sauce and place a fillet atop the sauce. Using a zigzag motion, drizzle a small amount of sauce over each fillet. Garnish with a sprig of fresh dill.

White wine butter sauce:
1 cup dry white wine
1 shallot, minced
2 tablespoons vinegar, preferably white wine
½ cup heavy cream
6 tablespoons (¾ stick) butter, chilled
1 pinch fresh dill

In a small saucepan, combine wine, shallot and vinegar. Bring to boil. Cook until syrupy and reduced to 2 tablespoons, about 10 minutes. Add cream and return to a boil. Cook until reduced by half (to about ¼ cup), about 8 minutes. Strain sauce and return to saucepan. Return to a boil, then remove from heat. Add butter (1 tablespoon at a time), whisking until each addition is melted and smooth. Stir in a pinch of fresh dill.

Hawaiian Cream Fruit Salad

Makes 8 to 10 Servings

1   (20-ounce) can pineapple tidbits, drained
1   (11-ounce) can mandarin orange segments, drained
1   (16-ounce) can peach slices, drained
1   (16-ounce) can pear slices, drained
1   apple
1   banana
1   (3.4-ounce) package vanilla instant pudding mix
1½   cups milk
⅓   (6-ounce) can frozen orange juice concentrate
¾   cup sour cream

Cut drained canned fruit and fresh fruit into bite-size pieces and place in a large bowl. Set aside.

In a small bowl, beat together pudding mix, milk and orange juice concentrate for 2 minutes. Add sour cream and mix thoroughly. Pour pudding mixture over fruit and stir to coat. Cover and refrigerate at least 2 hours.

Chewy Molasses Crinkles

Makes About 36 Cookies

¾	cup shortening or margarine, room temperature
1	cup plus ¼ cup sugar
¼	cup molasses
1	egg
2	cups flour
2	teaspoons baking soda
1	teaspoon cinnamon
½	teaspoon ground cloves
½	teaspoon ground ginger
½	teaspoon salt

In a large bowl, beat together shortening, 1 cup of sugar, molasses and egg. Sift in flour, baking soda, cinnamon, cloves, ginger and salt. Mix well and chill for at least 30 minutes.

Preheat oven to 375°F. Put ¼ cup of sugar in a small bowl. Form dough into 1-inch balls and roll in sugar. Place balls on a greased cookie sheet. Press fingertip in center of each, making a slight indentation. Bake for 8-10 minutes for a chewy cookie, or 10-12 minutes for a crisp cookie.

Northwest Eggs Benedict

Makes 4 to 6 Servings

8	eggs, hard-boiled and sliced
8	spears fresh asparagus, steamed until tender (or canned)
2-4	ounces smoked salmon, flaked
1½	sticks (¾ cup) butter or margarine
¾	cup flour
6	cups milk
1½	cups grated cheddar cheese (optional)

Salt and pepper, to taste
Paprika
Biscuits, cornbread or thick slices of toast

Preheat oven to 350°F. Coat 4 (16-ounce) custard cups or individual casserole dishes (for large servings), or 6 (12-ounce) cups (for smaller servings), with nonstick cooking spray. Divide egg slices equally among the dishes, followed by asparagus spears (cut asparagus into bite-size pieces, if desired). Sprinkle with flaked salmon.

Melt butter in a medium saucepan over medium heat. Stir in flour. Add milk gradually, stirring constantly (a wire whisk works well) until thick and smooth. Add cheese, if desired, and stir until melted. Season with salt and pepper. Divide sauce between individual dishes and sprinkle with paprika. Bake for 25-30 minutes, or until heated and bubbly. Serve with biscuits, cornbread or toast.

Rolled Smoked Ham, Spinach and Gruyère Omelet

Makes 4 Servings

You can substitute anything in this easy recipe, and what a way to do omelets — no fuss, no mess! For a colorful presentation, serve with a slice of cantaloupe and several bright red strawberries. A bagel or muffin completes the meal.

½   **cup flour**
1   **cup milk**
2   **tablespoons butter, melted**
½   **teaspoon salt**
4   **eggs**
1   **cup chopped smoked ham**
1   **small onion (or 1 leek or 5 green onions), chopped**
1½   **cups grated Gruyère or Swiss cheese**
1   **cup chopped fresh spinach leaves**
4   **large, whole spinach leaves, for serving**

Preheat oven to 350°F. Line a 15x10-inch jelly-roll pan with aluminum foil, making sure the foil goes all the way up all 4 sides of pan. Generously coat foil with nonstick cooking spray (do not use butter as it will burn and egg mixture will stick).

Using food processor or blender, blend flour, milk, butter, salt and eggs. Pour into prepared pan. Sprinkle evenly with ham and onions. Bake until eggs are set, about 15-18 minutes. Remove from oven and immediately sprinkle with cheese and spinach. Beginning at narrow end of the omelet, roll up, using foil to help lift and roll omelet.

To serve: Arrange 1 whole spinach leaf on each serving plate. Cut rolled omelet into 8 slices (each approximately 1¼-inches thick) and place 2 slices on each plate atop the spinach leaf.

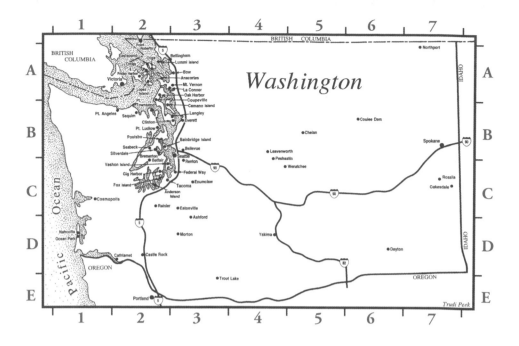

B&B Locations

Alphabetical Listing of B&Bs

Index

About the Authors

Carol McCollum Faino, an Iowa native and former teacher, started cooking as a young girl. Her creative cooking efforts were first publicly recognized when she received the Home Economics Superintendent's Award as a high school senior. She devoted much time to perfecting these winning skills by attending cooking classes, while raising three children, teaching and moving 15 times in 34 years (with 5 of those years spent in Washington state) with her husband, a retired Navy pilot. Carol and her husband, Rod, enjoy traveling, seeking out new bed & breakfasts and collecting simple, yet sensational recipes. They reside in Castle Rock, Colorado.

Doreen Kaitfors Hazledine is a former Mrs. South Dakota who traveled extensively, gave inspirational speeches and was named an Outstanding Young Woman of America. Before starting a writing career, she was a teacher and businesswoman and was listed as an honored professional in the National Register's WHO's WHO in Executives and Professionals. Her varied writing talents range from travel writing to inspirational nonfiction to screenwriting. A Hollywood producer optioned one of her screenplays.

Carol and Doreen are the authors of the *Washington State Bed & Breakfast Cookbook, Colorado Bed & Breakfast Cookbook*, the *California Wine Country Bed & Breakfast Cookbook and Travel Guide*.

3D Press Book Catalog

Boulder Cooks
Recipes and Profiles from Boulder County's Best Kitchens
$18.95 / 204pp / ISBN 0-9634607-8-1

Denver Hiking Guide
45 Hikes within 45 Minutes of Denver
$12.95 / 104pp / ISBN 1-889593-58-3

Colorado Bed & Breakfast Cookbook
From the Warmth & Hospitality of 88 Colorado B&B's and
Country Inns
$19.95 / 320pp / ISBN 0-9653751-0-2

Colorado Farmers' Market Cookbook
200 Recipes Fresh From Colorado's Farmers' Markets & Chefs
$18.95 / 224pp / ISBN 1-889593-00-1

Colorado Month-to-Month Gardening
A Practical Guide for Designing, Growing and Maintaining
Your Colorado Garden
$19.95 / 162pp / ISBN 1-889593-01-X

High Altitude Baking
175+ Recipes for Perfect Cakes, Breads, Cookies & More
Abover 5,000 Feet
$12.95 / 168pp / ISBN 1-889593-06-0

Month-to-Month Gardening Utah
Tips for Designing, Growing and Maintaining Your Utah Garden
$16.95 / 156pp / ISBN 1-889593-03-6

Month-to-Month Gardening New Mexico
$16.95 / 156pp / ISBN 1-889593-02-8

Washington State Bed & Breakfast Cookbook
From the Warmth & Hospitality of 85 B&B's and Country
Inns throughout Washington State.
$19.95 / 320pp / ISBN 1-889593-05-2

3D Press Order Form

4340 E. KENTUCKY AVE., SUITE 446
DENVER, CO 80246
888-456-3607

PLEASE SEND ME:	Price	Quantity
BOULDER COOKS	$18.95	_____
COLORADO BED & BREAKFAST COOKBOOK	$19.95	_____
COLORADO FARMERS' MARKET COOKBOOK	$18.95	_____
COLORADO MONTH-TO-MONTH GARDENING	$19.95	_____
DENVER HIKING GUIDE	$12.95	_____
HIGH ALTITUDE BAKING	$12.95	_____
MONTH-TO-MONTH GARDENING UTAH	$16.95	_____
MONTH-TO-MONTH GARDENING UTAH	$16.95	_____
WASHINGTON BED & BREAKFAST COOKBOOK	$19.95	_____

SUBTOTAL: $_____

Colorado residents add 3.8% sales tax. $_____

Add $5.00 for shipping for 1st book, add $1 for each additional $_____

TOTAL ENCLOSED: $_____

SEND TO:

Name_____

Address _____

City _____State _____Zip _____

Gift From _____

We accept checks, money orders, Visa or Mastercard (please include expiration date). Please make checks payable to 3D Press, Inc. Sorry, no COD orders.

Please charge my ☐ VISA ☐ MASTERCARD

Card Number _____ Expiration Date_____

Cardholder's Signature _____

CALL TOLL FREE 888-456-3607 FOR MORE INFORMATION

3D Press Book Catalog

Boulder Cooks
Recipes and Profiles from Boulder County's Best Kitchens
$18.95 / 204pp / ISBN 0-9634607-8-1

Denver Hiking Guide
45 Hikes within 45 Minutes of Denver
$12.95 / 104pp / ISBN 1-889593-58-3

Colorado Bed & Breakfast Cookbook
From the Warmth & Hospitality of 88 Colorado B&B's and Country Inns
$19.95 / 320pp / ISBN 0-9653751-0-2

Colorado Farmers' Market Cookbook
200 Recipes Fresh From Colorado's Farmers' Markets & Chefs
$18.95 / 224pp / ISBN 1-889593-00-1

Colorado Month-to-Month Gardening
A Practical Guide for Designing, Growing and Maintaining Your Colorado Garden
$19.95 / 162pp / ISBN 1-889593-01-X

High Altitude Baking
175+ Recipes for Perfect Cakes, Breads, Cookies & More Abover 5,000 Feet
$12.95 / 168pp / ISBN 1-889593-06-0

Month-to-Month Gardening Utah
Tips for Designing, Growing and Maintaining Your Utah Garden
$16.95 / 156pp / ISBN 1-889593-03-6

Month-to-Month Gardening New Mexico
$16.95 / 156pp / ISBN 1-889593-02-8

Washington State Bed & Breakfast Cookbook
From the Warmth & Hospitality of 85 B&B's and Country Inns throughout Washington State.
$19.95 / 320pp / ISBN 1-889593-05-2

3D Press Order Form

4340 E. KENTUCKY AVE., SUITE 446
DENVER, CO 80246
888-456-3607

PLEASE SEND ME:	Price	Quantity
BOULDER COOKS	$18.95	_____
COLORADO BED & BREAKFAST COOKBOOK	$19.95	_____
COLORADO FARMERS' MARKET COOKBOOK	$18.95	_____
COLORADO MONTH-TO-MONTH GARDENING	$19.95	_____
DENVER HIKING GUIDE	$12.95	_____
HIGH ALTITUDE BAKING	$12.95	_____
MONTH-TO-MONTH GARDENING UTAH	$16.95	_____
MONTH-TO-MONTH GARDENING UTAH	$16.95	_____
WASHINGTON BED & BREAKFAST COOKBOOK	$19.95	_____

SUBTOTAL: $_____

Colorado residents add 3.8% sales tax. $_____

Add $5.00 for shipping for 1st book, add $1 for each additional $_____

TOTAL ENCLOSED: $_____

SEND TO:

Name_____

Address _____

City _____ State _____ Zip _____

Gift From _____

We accept checks, money orders, Visa or Mastercard (please include expiration date). Please make checks payable to 3D Press, Inc. Sorry, no COD orders.

Please charge my ☐ VISA ☐ MASTERCARD

Card Number _____ Expiration Date_____

Cardholder's Signature _____

CALL TOLL FREE 888-456-3607 FOR MORE INFORMATION